Hair Today, Gone Tomorrow

By Pattie Parker

Hair Today, Gone Tomorrow

By Pattie Parker

Edited by Nathaniel Parker

Co-Edited and formatted by Gary Parker

Cover and Back Cover Design:

> Gary Parker and Gabriel Parker

Almost all photos by the author and her family

Published by:

Lulu online Publishing

http://www.lulu.com/

U.S.A.

Orders can be made online at
http://www.lulu.com/en/buy/?cid=en_tab_buy

Copyright © 2008

All rights reserved. No part of this book may be reproduced or transmitted in any form or by any means, electronic or mechanical, including photocopying, recording or by any information storage and retrieval system, without written permission from the author, except for the inclusion of brief quotations in review.

Dedication

I wonder how many people out there can say that they have worked the same job for more than thirty years; further, I wonder how many of those people cannot recall a single time during those thirty years when they wanted to be someplace else. Fortunately, I am one of those people. I wish to thank my husband, Gary, and my sons Gabriel and Nathaniel, for their unwavering support through all these years.

I would also like to dedicate this book to my sister and best friend, Kathy. Together, my family has inspired me and given me reason to always strive for success. I love you guys.

Cast of C-hair-actors

My name is Pattie Parker, and although the alliterative nature of my name might persuade you into thinking that I am a cartoon character, I assure you that I am not. I'm 57 years old, and have owned and operated the Progressive Barber Shop in Rochester, New York for more than 33 years.

I will be the first to tell you that I am not a professional writer; however, due to the constant encouragement from my loyal clientele and family, I feel compelled to share my incredible, albeit at times unbelievable, journey with you.

A few of the girls: Sue Kemp, Linda Stout, and me.

Although a wide variety of personalities will be revealed in the following pages, several have remained constant throughout my years at the Barber Shop. Many girls have worked with me over the years. Some of whom I consider my dearest friends. Sue, Roe, Linda, and Karen are as much a part of this book as I am. Without them, and without our zany collection of loyal clients (my husband and sons not excluded), there would be no story.

The Calling

I was attending St. Mary's catholic school in the coffee-stain town of Holley, New York when I heard the news of President Kennedy's death. What a time to be in the eighth grade. Sister Mary Celeste capitalized on this especially somber moment in order to reinforce what she thought it meant to be "called" toward the religious life. She preached about righteousness and dedication to God. I remember how sad her voice sounded over the loud speaker.

If you can believe it, not many of my grammar school classmates heard the religious "calling." Maybe the loud speaker wasn't working when the call came through. Remember, there was no *call-waiting* in 1963. Who knows?

In hindsight, I did have a sort of "calling" that year, but not to the religious life. I found out that year what kind of person I really was. According to the nuns at St. Mary's, I was an overly social little girl who rejected authority – and you did not need to be one of God's soldiers to see how right-on-the-money they were. Personally, I just saw myself as having the courage to do whatever, and get whatever it was that I wanted. Even back then, at thirteen years old, I knew that those same personality traits that the nuns loathed would determine the path that my life would take going into the future. And so, the stage was set.

No More Nuns

High school for me meant no more teachers dressed in black. No more being made to stand in the corner on one leg, hands and mouth duct taped shut. There would be no more beatings with what seemed to be a one hundred foot ruler. Ouch!

I would say that there was to be no more wondering if the nuns had shaved heads beneath their habits, but I still find myself wondering that, even today. So many times we tried to catch a glimpse as they stretched oh so high to erase the chalkboard, hoping, praying, to see just one stray little hair.

I saw high school as the big leagues. There was to be no more goofing around. It was all business now, serious. So, I found myself wondering how I was going to get through the next four years of my life with the littlest amount of effort. Non-regents, that was how!

What a beautiful thing! When you hate reading, studying can pose a real problem. Non-regents could greatly benefit a person like me. I would take fun classes like gym, music, and maybe homemaking (as it was called back then). Even the dumbest of the dumb could pass those classes, and so did I! I ended up pulling A's and B's in gym and music (as part of the Holley Hawks Marching Band), and got mostly D's in other subject areas. In my family, that was perfectly respectable. I was voted Class Treasurer and even deemed best dancer when I won a *twist* contest, of which the grand prize was the album "Silhouettes from the Shade" by Herman's Hermits.

By sophomore and junior year, things had not changed much. My social life was at a high; my grades were at a low. I was again voted Class Treasurer. That cracked me up. I didn't even know how to write a check, and here I was. Another picture in the yearbook! Go, girl!

Hair I Come

At the end of my junior year, Mr. McCarthy told me about a school called B.O.C.E.S. (Board of Cooperative Extension). After doing a little research on the matter, there were two things that really appealed to me about the B.O.C.E.S. program: One was it offered training in cosmetology, which was something that mildly interested me, and the second if I went, I would only have academic classes in the mornings…strictly hairdressing in the afternoons. Talk about the mother lode! How cool was this?! It would cost me thirty-five dollars to purchase my kit that would include my scissors, rollers, combs, and manicuring equipment.

Not to toot my own horn, but from day one, I pretty much aced every written and practical exam. (Did I mention that I have owned my shop for well over thirty years?) I found my calling!

I decided to enter the "Junior Miss Pageant," and one of my teachers convinced me to use my hairdressing skills for the talent portion of the contest. I would do these elaborate hair-dos on live models, and have them walk down the runway while I explained each hairstyle. I was probably the queerest thing I had ever done. I didn't even place.

In my defense, I do not think it was the hair thing that did it; more likely, it was the fact that I had to do my jazz dance without music when "The Girl from Ippinema" broke in the cassette player. I think that repeating the same basic dance step 300 times to a deafening silence did not much help matters. I freaked - I'll be the first to admit that. However, I could still out *twist* anyone.

It's a Comb…Not a Wand!

My senior year finally arrived. I was beginning to get very anxious about graduation, the prom, my future, and all the things that were yet to come. Soon after I graduated, I got a part-time job at a hair salon at the Greece Town Mall, working with real clients, as opposed to designated models in some teenybopper beauty pageant. This experience would prove to be a rude awakening.

Why do people have such unrealistic expectation? It is a question I have asked an infinite number of times throughout my career. Women would bring magazine pictures of movie stars like Marilyn Monroe and Audrey Hepburn, and request that we make them look like the people in their photographs. Hello. If it is a miracle you are looking for, you would have better luck taking a pilgrimage to Fatima. The whole

Street in the town of Brockport. I don't know who was more excited, my father (who had invested so much into my career), or me. It wasn't long before Tony saw how good I had become. I had men lined up at the door waiting for me! Tony was so pleased, and I loved going to work at his Barber Shop. Eighteen months flew by and I knew it was about time to move on. I would be taking my state board test before too long, and I had plans to move to a bigger city with a bigger clientele.

In August of 1971, my sister Kathy, two other girls and I moved to Averill Ave. in Rochester. I was the only one without a job. I didn't have a car or a license to drive the car that I did not have. As my father would say, I had two good legs though! Moreover, I put them to work. I walked up and down Monroe Avenue looking for gainful employment. After a week or two of looking, and still no paycheck coming in, I began to panic. I needed to find a job, and soon!

My Uncle Mike ended up turning me on to a barber who would let me work part-time in his shop. I took the job. At least now I would be able to contribute my portion of the rent.

One morning, I got up and prepared myself for a long walk to the new shop – which I couldn't find! Again, panic. You can imagine my frustration. I stopped into the Progressive Barber Shop to ask for directions, and wouldn't leave for the next thirty-three years.

The man at Progressive was Nick Valentino. His partner was Sam Jullian. In those days, there was also the shoeshine man, Mr. Sam. Mr. Sam, an old black man, would become one of my closest friends, and even now, thirty-something years later, and years past his death, his antique shoeshine kit still sits proudly in the corner of our Progressive Barber Shop.

"Can I help you?" Nick asked. He hired me on the spot. I would end up doing manicures and the occasional haircut for almost two years. Remember, there was not as much of a demand for haircuts in those days because, as you might have read, long hair was the style. For many reasons, I trusted Nick and Sam. I also knew that under their guidance, I would someday become a Master Barber, too. After all, these guys were very good. I would sit there, watching every new technique they used. I was like a sponge, soaking up everything they had to teach me. If I had to manicure for a while, so be it. The benefits in the end would be well worth it.

Although the atmosphere at Progressive was relaxed and fun, there were very clear morning rituals and responsibilities. You were to be there promptly at 8:00 AM. The coffee was to be put on immediately, and the newspaper crossword puzzle would be done. Only then would the work begin. Thirty-three years later, I still start my mornings in the same way – well, perhaps a little closer to 9…okay 10:00.

Nick would cut customers' hair, while I manicured and Mr. Sam shined shoes. We were like a finely oiled machine. If we had a break, Nick would have me practice shaving him, and in exchange, he would give me a hot-towel facial. I remember Nick had a very difficult face to shave. He had a very thick beard and a deep cleft in his chin. He also had a big mole on his right cheek. One false stroke with that straight razor, and he would have been wearing that mole on his chest. I figured if I could shave him, I could shave a baby made of tissue paper. Meanwhile, my complexion never looked so good! Needless to say, we both enjoyed our little arrangement.

Even though Nick and I traded shaves for facials, I still had to do my fair share of the facials when it came to the customers. Funny thing about giving facials, the customers are so relaxed because of the hot towels that they never know how close they come to being covered in vomit.

It used to gross me out big-time when I would have to grab the customers' nostrils and squeeze out their puss-filled pores, much like squeezing a zit. The hot towels would open the pores, thus making the escape much easier for the creamy goop trapped beneath the skin. At times, I remember there being countless tiny openings bubbling with white paste.

Another part of giving a facial that bothered me was removing in-grown hairs. Often, they swell up and tend to cause pain. Some of these suckers you'll find embedded a half an inch below the surface of the skin. The longer they grow, the more coiled they become. First thing, sterilize the needle. Secondly, dig. Break the skin, find the hair, and yank it out with a pair of tweezers. Not an easy task. If the customers were lucky, there would be minimal bloodshed. If they were lucky, there might not even be remnants of a scar. Hey, anything for a buck.

Don't Bug Me

This last story brings to mind another instance where giving a facial grossed me out. No worries, though, this one has nothing to do with puss, or blood, or face paste. It has to do with cockroaches.

One Saturday afternoon, I was giving this nice man a facial and a shave, when something in the corner of my eye caught my attention. About a million things were going through my mind as to what it might have been that I saw. Not wanting to alert the man in the chair below, I chose to ignore what I had seen. I put a hustle in the many services, trying to get him finished and out of the shop so I could further investigate. No dice.

Three more of the creatures scurried across the counter. I put another hot towel over the man's face so that I could investigate further without alarming him. COCKROACHES!! There was a full invasion happening right under our noses. I opened one of the drawers and there were four more of the not-so-little suckers. They must have been planning on taking over the shop. I could not let this happen, especially considering how far I had come.

The man left without incident and I immediately called the terminator, AKA my husband. We went to the serious animal killing store and bought way too much and far too potent, animal killing poison. The next morning, there were wall-to-wall quarter-sized black cadavers all over the shop. Victory was ours! Gary and I had successfully obliterated an entire colony of roaches, thus saving the shop.

Ashes to ashes, roaches to sleep, may the little buggers rest in peace.

A Close Shave

Remember how good I said I thought I was at barbering? I was now preparing to take the test for the second time. I flunked my first attempt. How nerve-racking an experience though, really! The test consisted of a haircut, a shave, a facial, and a series of questions asked by one of the judges, of which there are six. All of whom were Master Barbers.

I had felt confident going into the first test, but I ended up having trouble with one aspect of the test. I could not hone the straight razor as sharp as it needed to be. I think that, as well as my slow pace were determining factors in my failing. I was so depressed that I did not want to ever take the exam again. Nick would not have any of that though. He said that he had the solution to my problem. He would prepare me a razor ahead of time that was as sharp as the Devil, himself. I would keep that razor in my pocket, and when the time came to present a honed razor to the judges, I would secretly and swiftly switch them. No one would know! I passed that second test in record time.

I was now a ***Master Barber***.

Yes, Godfather

One of the craziest experiences I ever had in my early years as a Master Barber was joining the local barber's union shortly after I had passed the New York State test. Nick had suggested that it would be a good idea.

You've really got to appreciate this scene: Three hundred men, none of whom stood over 5'4" tall, gathered together like tightly packaged sausages in a basement where the only light was provided by hundreds of candles. Moreover, here I was, the only woman, wearing magenta hot pants and thigh-high suede boots.

Earlier that day, Nick had said to me that I probably would not be able to understand our union president because he spoke with such a deep Italian accent. If I were ever addressed, or asked a question, Nick told me to just, "Say yes." And that is just what I did. My boss escorted me to the podium to meet with Vito Corleone; and when it was over, I was quietly escorted back to my seat. I remember thinking that the applause that ensued lasted far too long. Anyway- that night I became an official member of the barbers union.

I paid monthly union dues for many years for reasons that I will never know. That is just what you did. In the years that followed, all the old timers either retired or died, and with them went the union. Amen. I was happy not having to pay my dues anymore.

The barber's union was not intended to help people like me. More specifically, it was not designed to benefit women. This makes perfect sense when you consider there were no women barbers at the time the union was created. When I got pregnant with my first son, the union did not intend to compensate me for the time I would have to take for maternity leave. In the original contract, there were no provisions for my situation. Being the self-designated advocate for feminism that I was, I went down to the union hall - and threw a hissy fit! Union contracts were amended that day. I guess you could say that I made old Vito Corleone an offer he couldn't refuse. I received my money one week later. Victory.

The Boys

As I have already mentioned, the barbering business back then was not what it is today. The popularity of long hair coupled with infrequent visits to the barbershop was affecting every barber in the city. For the most part, our clientele consisted mostly of Nick and Sam's friends coming in to play gin rummy all day long. The games would frequently last until closing time. I didn't mind the guys coming in all the time, though. For one thing, they were very nice, and I liked their company. Secondly, the more time Nick and Sam spent playing cards, the more opportunities I had to cut some hair.

Customers would become impatient waiting for them to finish a hand, and they would ask me if I wanted to cut them. Hell, yes! Finally, I got my chance to do what I had always wanted. Mr. Sam would shine shoes, Nick and Sam would play cards with the boys, and I would cut hair. Everyone was happy, especially me!

Nick and Sam would only occasionally cut some hair; but basically, Mr. Sam and I ran things around the shop. I understood their motives, though. The way the business was back then; Nick and Sam had more financial success playing gin all day.

I benefited from the guys playing gin all day, too. After I bought the shop, I began to charge them a modest fee for the use of the back room. The setup was sweet until their wives found out where and how they were spending their afternoons, and made them stop. Bummer! The nuns at the Blessed Sacrament Church inherited the table and chairs.

Time to Cut and Run

Around this time, Nick had begun selling real estate part-time. After about my third year at the shop, he and Sam offered me a deal to buy the shop. They told me that they wanted the famed Progressive Barber Shop to continue to exist and they felt they could entrust me with the business they had owned and run for so long. Nick and Sam had owned Progressive for about thirty years, and the original owners (Milt Axlerod and Herman Casanov) had owned it for thirty years before them.

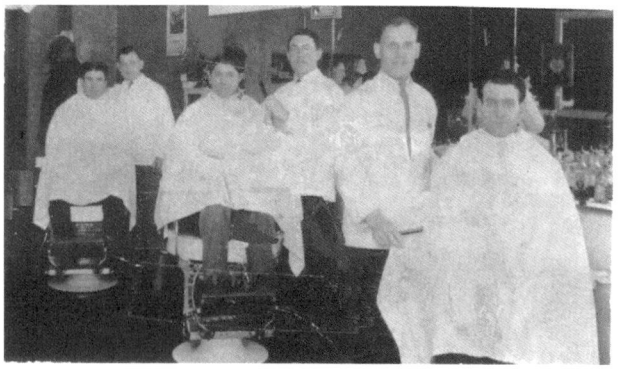

The original shop

For about sixty years, the Progressive Barber Shop was an institution in the city. I understood why Sam and Nick wanted to pass it on to me. And why wouldn't I buy it? I loved what they had, and now had the opportunity to have it all for myself. There was one minor problem, though. Money. I had none.

I suppose I could have gotten the money from Nick and Sam's gin buddies, but I ended up getting a loan from the bank – God only knows how. I'm not one to look a gift horse in the mouth, however, so I took the loan in February of 1974 and officially took over the shop on March 3, 1974. I was twenty-four years old.

The first thing I did was I renovated. I applied for incentive laden Rochester City Business Grants and redid the entire interior and the exterior of the old building. Coincidentally, Mr. Sam decided to retire his old shoeshine kit. He was in his seventies and was starting to slow down. I was very sad to see him leave, but we both knew we would always remain good friends. I eventually did hire someone to fill his shoes (no pun intended), but nobody could ever replace him. Sam was the man.

Interestingly enough, almost two decades later, my youngest son Nathaniel would use the same shoeshine kit that Mr. Sam left behind to shine the shoes of a whole new base of customers. Nathaniel was eleven years old.

Opening for Business---Alone!?

It felt weird showing up for work alone. I remember feeling sad and excited at the same time. There was no longer anyone to have the morning coffee with; no longer anyone to do the morning crossword puzzle with; and no longer anyone to say, "Mornin' Miss Pattie." I was a little intimidated being on my own.

Max was the first customer that ever came into *my* shop. Max was one of the card players, and it delighted me to see a familiar face. Even though he was familiar to me, I still had the shakes for some reason. It would be fine, though.

The next customer was a new guy. He walked in carrying a box under his arm. I was a little scared thinking that it might be a human head or something else just as creepy. It turned out to be not as creepy, but just as strange. The man had a box, within which was a toupee-a hairpiece-a rug! Even more strangely, yet, he wanted me to take a little off the top of it! I remember thinking "Is this guy nuts-o?" I did it, though; and it quite honestly looked great. In case you were wondering, I did charge him full price.

One day Sid, a card player and regular client, wanted me to give him a shave. Having practiced on Nick all the time had me feeling ultra confidant. Things were going quite well when Sid decides to ask me a question just as I was gliding the straight razor across his chin. Talk about blood. I had to use an entire tube of styptic powder and half dozen cold towels to plug that gash. Sid was Mr. Cool, though-bless his soul. I was having a coronary and *he* was apologizing to *me*!

On another occasion, I accidentally nipped off a guy's right earlobe. Did you know that the fatty part of an earlobe does not have a lot of blood in it? It's just kind of hollow in there. I know because the part that I had severed from his ear was sitting there, lifeless, on his cape. That sucked. Just as Sid had, this gentleman remained extraordinarily calm, as well. He showed up at my wedding soon after with a big bandage over his victim ear. I'm not sure who was more embarrassed – him or me.

Above all else, though, if there is one bit of advice you should take away from this part of my story, it is to stay away from noses whenever possible. I'm not going to get into detail, but I will say that no amount of styptic powder and cold towels will ever be enough to stop the flow of a billion blood-gushing capillaries. Ick!

I can only imagine what the repercussions would have been if these customers had been women. I would imagine that a woman who comes to the barber for a shave might have quite a temper. Seriously, though, the thing about men is they are more likely to grin, bear it, and forgive honest mistakes.

Help Un-Wanted

As the popularity of long hair died down, people began going to the barber again. Business was so good that I had to hire help. Mostly all the girls who I have hired to help at the shop have ended up staying several years because it is such a fun, relaxing work environment. Almost all of the girls have ended up being reliable, trustworthy, and ethical. But…there have been exceptions.

One such horror story involved a girl who worked for me for more than eight years. It's a long time, I know! And I did trust her. The only problem I had with her was she used to dress a little too risqué for the shop. Oh! She didn't do a very good haircut either; but that is neither here nor there. On a couple of occasions, I had to send her home to change her clothes. We were, after all, women working mostly with men. In a business like ours, you did not want to invite any unnecessary trouble. She turned out to be trouble in the end, though.

In the late 1980's, I moved the location of the shop up the Avenue a little way because of the crime and the building lease price. When I moved the shop, she stayed. She did not even tell me she was going to stay. One day, she was just gone. As it turns out, she had been planning on taking over my old building for some time. She had even been passing out her new business cards while she was still working for me in *my* shop. Talk about unethical.

When customers who were not aware of my move asked her where I had gone, she would tell them all kinds of crazy stories. Either I was out on medical leave, or I had retired, or I was on an extended vacation. Meanwhile, I was about a quarter mile down the Avenue on the same side of the road!

My customers are so great, though. One day soon after all this stuff went down, Shel, one of my dearest friends and clients, showed up at my shop with a head full of soaking wet hair. When I asked him what had happened, he told me that he was actually sitting in the chair at the other shop when he figured out what had happened between the other barber and me. He had stood up in the middle of his cut, tore off his haircloth, and walked down Monroe Avenue to find me. I'll bet he drove, but God bless him, anyway.

Make no mistake, though, there were other hiring disasters besides this one. One of my ladies, unbeknownst to me, turned out to be a raging nymphomaniac. According to several---let's just say *reliable* sources, she would play Madam of the

Barber Shop at all hours of the night with a barrage of men of all ages, colors and sizes. I spent weeks sterilizing the chairs after I let her go.

One morning, soon after being forced to fire this girl for conduct unbecoming of the shop, I found a fresh serving of feces and a pail of cool urine waiting for me at the doorway. Classy.

The girl I hired to take the sex-maniac's place cut hair really well, actually. Too bad she lived only one block away and never once made it to work on time. Plus, she had the personality of a slug. Working with her was like being in an oil painting of a mortuary. Needless to say, her tenure was short lived.

Hairy Situations

You may recall that in the late seventies and early eighties, Afros were the craze. I convinced my boyfriend at the time to let me perm his hair. Hesitantly, he agreed. That was our first mistake. The next mistake, however, was all me. Something went terribly wrong with the process and his hair ended up looking like Doc Brown in back to the future. You could almost hear people's thoughts as he passed by them. "Has that guy been electrocuted?" It was so bad, that I would actually avoid being seen with him. After some bargaining,

I got him to let me attempt to reverse the perm. Big Mistake! The combination of chemicals resulted in clumps of hair falling out by the handful. To this day, that man, my husband of 33 years, blames his baldness on me. Ain't love grand?

I do not usually work on Saturdays. Coincidentally, that is when some of the biggest Boo-Boos happen – like the day Ro, one of my long-time girls, thinned this guy's ear. Confused? Allow me to explain.

Thinning scissors are like regular cutting scissors, but with teeth, so they only cut half the surface area of the blade. When cutting hair, which is what they were intended to cut, the hair becomes less dense, or thinned. But when cutting an ear, the result is something much more tragic. Oh well, Ro, at least it didn't land in his lap, right?

Linda is something else, as well. She has been with me for a very long time; and you would think that in all that time, she would have learned that she is one of those people who cannot walk and chew gum at the same time. You can imagine what could happen if you mixed cutting hair with conversation. Travesty.

On several occasions, the phone at the shop has rung and on the other end of the line was a man who had noticed that only half his head had been cut. You might ask why he had not noticed sooner. The answer is he did not notice at all…his wife did. There is yet another example of the easygoingness of men.

Jim is a loyal customer of mine and one of my great friends. It is important to mention that I have never seen Jim without a full and hearty beard. I had been having one of those bad days and, let me tell you, I had a hell of a time convincing Jim how good he looked without that beard. Oops!

He Got Clipped

Some of the most memorable experiences I have had have come as the result of clipper fiascos. As is the case with most things, they just don't make clippers the way they used to. Take the plastic ends as an example. Back in the day, clipper heads used to be made out of steel and were attached to the clipper blade by an impenetrable buckle. You never had to worry about the head falling off the clipper (although the threat of tetanus was not so unrealistic). I am sure making clipper heads out of plastic and making them more easily changeable is cost affective for the manufacturers, but it comes with problems on our end.

The way clippers work is like this: there are different heads that can be put on the end of the clipper blade in order to determine the length of the hair being cut. A *#1* clipper head will cut hair as short as ¼ inch, whereas a *#5* head will leave hair over an inch long. Customers understand this, and often times they know exactly what clipper head they want. Tom knew.

One of my long time customers, known in the shop simply as Tom from (the town) of Chili, comes in for an appointment, and asks me for a 'number 4' on top and a 'number 2' on the sides – a longer version of the high-and-tight military cut sounds fine, right?

So I'm standing there talking Tom's ear off (as per usual), when *BBBbbbzzzzzzzzzzz!* I look down and old Tom has a 2 X 3" patch of scalp looking up at me from the side of his head. The headpiece of the clipper popped off as I was going in for a cut, and the bare blade of the clipper practically shaved him.

Now remember, Tom has no idea what has just occurred, seeing as how he has no angle to view the mistake. You might have thought my sudden silence would have tipped him off that something had gone terribly wrong, but I think he was just thankful to have had a moment of silence. I continued cutting his hair, silently thinking about how to go about telling him what had just happened.

After careful deliberation, I decided to try to convince him that he should let me make his hair shorter considering the upcoming warm spell we were sure to be getting. It did not work. Maybe I won't charge him, I remember thinking. No - that would be a sure giveaway that something had happened. Maybe I should just fess up. I know, I thought that was a stupid idea, too. Finally, the answer I had been searching for hit me right on the head. I would do nothing at all. Worst-case scenario would be that I lose a good customer; best-case scenario is that he and his wife never notice and it is never even an issue. As soon as he left, the guilt consumed me.

A week later, Tom returns. Before he can even speak a word, I'm confessing like he is my priest. I fix his haircut, offer him two free-bees and immediately feel at peace. The funny thing about the whole story is that it was his co-workers that finally noticed, not Tom or his wife. I am unsure how to interpret that.

A similar thing had happened a few years before the Tom incident. It happened when I was giving my son a haircut. That little mistake ended up costing me a $25 dollar Pittsburg Steelers hat. Nathaniel was a little cleverer, though. He realized what had happened, extorted the hat out of me, and told the kids at school that he had slipped at Thanksgiving dinner, hit his head on the corner of the kitchen table, and the hospital had to shave his head in that little spot in order to give him stitches. Kids say the darnedest things.

Hair here, Hair there, Hair everywhere

I have always wondered why men lose the hair on their heads, only to have it sprout up on other areas of their bodies – exotic areas. I have seen such thick nose hair on a man that at first glance you would no doubt mistake it for part of their moustache. I have seen ear hair so dense that it had actually wrapped itself around their hearing aide. I have seen eyebrows that could be used as comb-overs.

What I do not understand is why some guys refuse to have this overabundance of hair trimmed or neatened up. Are these men wolf men? Will they lose their super powers if they groom their facial orifices?

What if women let their chin hairs flourish, without removing or bleaching it? What if we chose to flaunt our moustaches? Guys, am I getting through to you?

The Bald and the Beautiful

As is the case usually, people are never happy with the hand that God has dealt them. This fact is especially prevalent when it comes to men and their hair. Gentlemen (and I use that term loosely) who have hair seem not to want it, whereas men without hair want nothing more. Young men with gorgeous heads of hair come into the shop all the time wanting one of the girls to BIC their heads bald. Other men, with two or three stragglers on top, seem to want to keep their scarce hair in hopes that after eating magical beans, or rubbing some Gypsy potion on their heads, those few hairs will procreate, multiplying.

Further, men with curly hair pay to have their hair straightened, while men with straight hair pay to have it permed. I am convinced that God separates people from their *hair identities* before they are born, leaving people feeling like hairy fishes-out-of-water. It would be a travesty if I weren't the one making a profit from the whole deal. Cha-ching!

Hair Today, Gone Tomorrow

Hairstyles come and go. Like clothes, what was popular twenty years ago will be popular again. Hairstyles like the Princeton, the flat top, and the brush cut go in and out of style continuously. I will say it can be depressing when you see a hairstyle become popular for the third time. That is when you notice how old you're getting. Ugh!

One of the more recent hairstyles - and due to the stressors involved in creating it, one of my least favorite - is the *custom carve*. This is when a customer will come in and ask me (or one of the girls) to carve a letter, or a shape, or a treasure map where X marks the spot in the back of their heads.

These projects are so nerve-racking because of the steady hand necessary to succeed. After all, once something is shaved into your hair, there is only one way to erase it…and aftershave on the scalp burns badly.

This little boy came into the shop once wanting me to shave a capital letter 'G' in the back of his head. It came out great, too! I even convinced him to let me color it in with a green magic marker I had. Awesome! The next day, his mother, obviously upset, called me and told me that I had used permanent marker on her son's hair. I had no idea. What could I say? "It will grow out"…CLINK.

Then there was the Moe Howard bowl cut, where the hair on the sides of the man's head was short, but on top, it looked like a mushroom cap. How foolish. This cut always reminds me of an oversized and permanent Jewish yarmulke. Either way, like the colored Mohawk and the cult-classic mullet, the Moe Howard bowl cut went out of style.

Ironically, some of the most ridiculous cuts we have ever had to do have ended up being some of our coolest. Anyone who was alive to witness the legacy of the Buffalo Bills of the early nineties will appreciate this story. A younger guy came into my shop after losing a football bet with some of his coworkers. He had to get the Buffalo Bills icon shaved into the back of his head. Mind you, my shop employs a bunch of women, not at all familiar with the Buffalo Bills, let alone their team logo. All he had for us to follow was a crude picture.

Out of fear, I refused to do it, so one of my girls, Sue, got the honor. It came out perfect. I was in awe. She even painted on the Buffalo Bill's red, white, and blue (with non-permanent markers this time)! This was a rare request, and it came out better than any of us could have hoped.

Not a week later, another young man came into the shop. He had seen the Bills logo, and liked it so much that he wanted to have a volleyball carved into the top of his head. Volleyball! He must have talked to the other guy, because he also came equipped with a picture for us to go by. I kept thinking to myself as this guy was telling us what he wanted, one false move and this guy would have a football instead of volleyball. I gave this client to Linda, another one of my long-time girls. Again, it came out beautifully: another happy customer.

If things like this happen in threes, I am still waiting for a hunter to come in and want us to carve his latest kill into the side of his noggin

Talk about trophy heads!

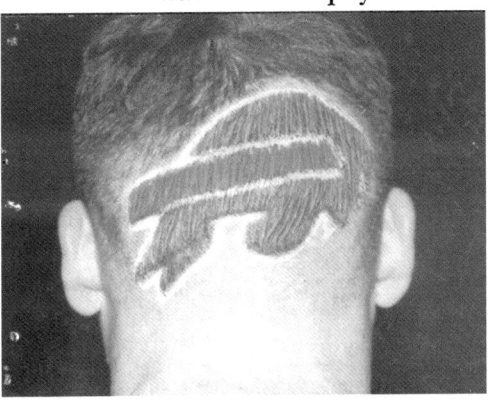

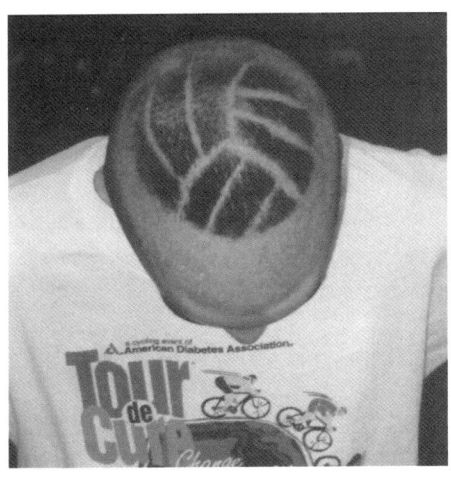

Nod for Nothin'

It has always baffled me how some customers can so easily fall asleep beneath a

Dave getting comfortable

stranger with a razor-sharp pair of scissors and a fifty year old set of eyes. Nonetheless, some customers find getting a haircut to be a very relaxing experience. Some of them snore; some of their heads teeter back and forth like bobble head dolls. With all this going on, you have to hold their heads with one hand and clipper-cut with the other, all the time considering that if you were to lose a grip for just a moment, their heads might flop, and *snap*, a broken neck! I have never had the stomach to be able to *Sweeny Todd* a customer.

I wish more people would see the glaring similarities between getting a haircut and suffering a severe concussion - falling asleep could be deadly. Meat pies anyone?

Parents say the darnedest things

Through the years, I have had the pleasure of giving "first haircuts" to countless youngsters, many of whom I have also witnessed grow into outstanding young men. I went to school to be a barber, however, and not a teacher; and on many occasions, when I have to negotiate with youngsters and their parents, I am reminded why.

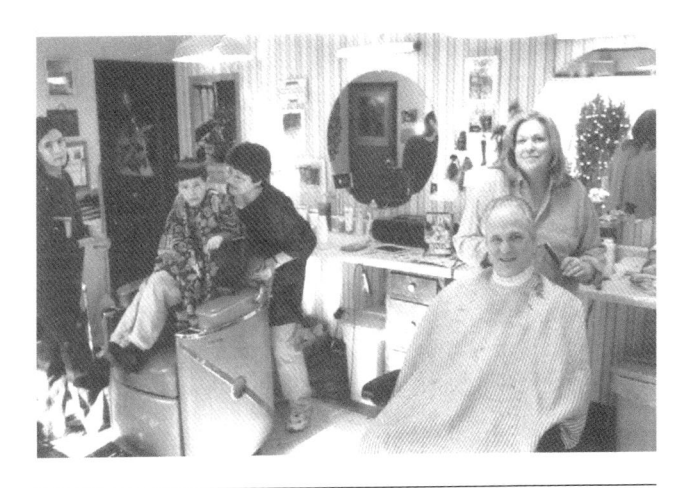

Could anyone out there please tell me why young parents would decide to bring their children in for a haircut either right before naptime or right after they have woken up? It is during those times that a trained eye can detect the subtle signs a child practices when sitting still for the barber is not on the top of their *favorite-things-to-do* list.

Most parents will not be dissuaded by their children's' unwillingness to cooperate, however. moms and dads are usually so determined to get little Johnny's hair cut that they will resort to actually restraining the kid with hand-shackles, actually holding their ankles and wrists down, making them as still as possible so we barbers can do our worst, which is usually how these haircuts turn out, anyway.

Amidst the piercing screams from the children, you can count on moms saying something along the lines of, "Grandma will be so happy to see your beautiful haircut!" Between you and me, the way this haircut is going to turn out, grandma might as well have done it herself.

Then there are the parents who sit their child down in the chair and ask them how they would like their haircut. The kid is all of two years old, and has a vocabulary consisting of no more than half-a-dozen words, and they honestly expect their child to be able to articulate his preferred hairstyle! (Place expletive here!)

One kid actually told me, in front of his parents, that he wanted to rip off my head and stuff it down my neck. Parenting at its best, I say…especially if you're raising a serial killer. The worst part of this story is that same kid grew up to be a bigger creep as an adult. I only pray that he liked a few of the haircuts he got when he was a toddler. Seriously, though, if you ever arrive at the shop for an appointment and find me dead, with my head stuffed down my neck, consider this chapter a clue.

Every Dog has its Day

The famous picture of the world's coolest dog

Sometimes the Progressive Barbershop appears to be more like a kennel for a motley cross-section of pups. When I first bought the shop, I had a Sheepdog mix named Pepper. Pepper went to work with me almost every day for eighteen years, when we finally had to put him down.

Pepper was a longhaired shaggy dog, not unlike many of my customers in the late seventies. I would cut his hair between appointments with clients. Sometimes, it would take me all day - a little here, a little there. Somewhere in a New York City Museum, there hangs a picture of Pepper in the front window of the original shop before we moved.

An aspiring photographer took a picture of him years ago, and apparently, someone thought he was photogenic. I did too! These days, Pepper is gone, and the two dogs I have now are too ornery to bring to work every day. There are, however, a plethora of neighborhood dogs that visit me daily. There's Caesar, Peanut, Hubcap, Rocky, Smokey, Kayla, Diesel, Abe, Birdie, Maggie, Lucy, Walker, Frenchy, Queenie, Liz Oliver, and Monty, just to name a few.

It is not just the visiting pooches that make the shop seem like more of a kennel sometimes. The girls and I have several times saved abused and homeless puppies from grave fates. Karen, one of my girls and sister-in-law, found the tiniest little pup wandering around by herself at Cobb's Hill Park, just up the road from the shop. The puppy was some type of Pitt Bull mix. She was obviously malnourished and scared half to death. There was little doubt she had been abused.

After a bit of coaxing, Karen was able to lure the young puppy into her truck and brought her back to the shop. After a few weeks of TLC, and a few trips to the vet, the little pup started acting like a little angel, the perfect pet. We kept her at the shop during the day (and at Karen's at night), and everyone who met her wanted to take her home with them. Before we would let her go, however, we were determined to find the right family for her. After all, she was our little girl, and she depended on us, now.

After about three months, we thought we had found a good fit for *Pepper*, as we began to call her. The man sounded very sincere in wanting the dog, and expressed to us how much he loved her personality, so we gave Pepper to him. We were devastated. Only a dog owner can understand the bond that is inevitably formed between a parent and their dog. If you are wondering why we could not keep her, ourselves, it is because we both already owned two dogs…and BIG dogs, for that matter. We were content, however, that Pepper was going to a good home and that her owner would take good care of her.

Not more than twenty minutes after Pepper had left the shop with her new owner, we heard a bark coming from outside the shop door. It was Pepper! She had escaped the man's yard and ran back to the shop. She did it twice that day, and Karen and I decided that it was Pepper's way of telling us that she was not entirely satisfied with her new owner. He must have been convinced, too, because he sadly gave her back to us.

Soon after that whole debacle, we did find a very special person to adopt Pepper. She was a sweet elderly woman who brings her grandson into the shop to get his hair cut. As soon as they met the dog, there was an instant connection. Everybody knew it was a perfect fit, even Pep. That was a few years ago, now, and that once dejected and neglected little puppy now has more love and attention than it knows what to do with. Now that is a doggone happy ending!

But before ending this chapter, I would be remiss if I didn't mention that **all** my hairy friends get treats with every visit. I go through more doggie biscuits than I do hair products, but that's ok. I love it! It does get a little disconcerting though when a client (I'll call him Frank) comes in for a haircut, a cup of coffee and a ***liver flavored dog biscuit***! He eats them like it was his last meal. Even the canines look at him with disgust and amazement. I tell you, I'm sure that he lifts his leg to pee and barks at his wife when he wants a treat.

Get on your knees

Because I have so many plants in my barber shop, a lot of my clients ask if they can take snippings of them to plant at home. No problem, but *they* have to cut them. (Most of them are cacti). I remember one guy kneeling on the floor, fighting with one of these cacti. After a few minutes, he stood up and noticed a wet spot on his knee. After a bit of silence, I caught a glimpse of a flat, hairy splotch on my carpet. It had a long string attached to it. Dang! The guy had knelt down, and squished a tiny little innocent mouse. His little guts were all mashed together. Ugh! The poor little thing didn't have a squeak of a chance. I scrapped the little carcass up and threw it into Linda's garbage, anxiously awaiting her arrival. Remember the cowboy boots? How I love to torment her. Oops, I prematurely gave away a hint at coming attractions you'll read about later.

Tricks of the Trade

A barbershop is a perfect place to play and enjoy practical jokes – especially when said barbershop is owned by yours truly. As you might imagine, the way that people react to practical jokes, no matter how innocent and tasteful they seemed at the time, can be very different depending on the vict…err…person. In a barbershop, where the clientele is extraordinarily diverse both personally and politically, playful gags tend to take on a personality all their own.

It was Halloween, 1993. Moseying through a local costume shop, I came across a very eerie and real-looking rubber rat about the size of a Schnauzer. How fun! I figured I could find this disgusting little guy a home beneath the sink in the bathroom at the shop. Moreover, to ensure that he would not run away, I thought I would pin his delicate little neck beneath the cold steel of an oversized rattrap.

My baby rodent!

Almost immediately after placing the vermin in its new home, I got my first victim. We were all busy cutting, and with the loud humming of the clippers and the hair driers and the television, none of us heard her go into the bathroom. After a few minutes or so, the hair driers stopped, the clippers shut down, and the TV volume was lowered. The droning hum of the three was replaced by the hysterical sobs of a 9-year-old girl. She had walked into the bathroom, seen the puppy-sized rat in the rusty trap and melted down. I think what really drove her over the edge was the tiny motor inside the creature that caused it to twitch and squirm when she got too close to it. I couldn't help but feel partially responsible for the little girl's trauma that day.

The success of the first prank only fed my desire to do it again. I did what any business owner would do at that point; I called my landlords. I told them that there had been weird noises coming from the bathroom, and I was afraid to go in and check it out by myself. They came in at the perfect time. The shop was wall-to-wall with customers. Going over to the bathroom, they slowly opened the bathroom door, and peeked inside. Slam!

They immediately closed the door, red with fear and uncertainty.

"Pattie, we have a bit of a problem," they said as calmly as possible, "We'll be right back."

"What is it?" I said.

They replied, "Trust us; you do not want to see."

A few minutes later, the two of them returned with a garbage bag and a club. It was at that point that bellowing laughter exploded in the

Somebody pulled my tail! A customer holds our rat-friend prior to its unfortunate demise.

barbershop. When Dave and Gene were let in on the little joke, I honestly think they wanted to turn their club on me; but they would have needed a bigger garbage bag. It was a sad day when we had to throw out our little rodent friend. Sometime soon after, a customer had come into the shop and overflowed the toilet, getting "ickies" on him. Yuck! Needless to say, he had to go.

More Antics

Several years ago, there was a hole in the ceiling at the barber shop, and I was mad at my husband for postponing the reparations, so I decided to fix *him* instead. I set up a lunch date and told him to meet me at the shop early in the afternoon. That morning I fixed him a gourmet meal of bologna and spackle on white bread.

Now mind you, my co – worker Sue was genuinely concerned that he would actually eat the sandwich and get sick. It did not concern me because my husband is very rigid in his diet. He always inspects his meal before he eats. Always.?

Having apparently missed breakfast, Gary bit into his lunch fearlessly and famishedly. Sue immediately buried her head into a magazine, trying to conceal her nervous laughter. In hindsight, I suppose I could have been quicker to inform him that he had just eaten spackle, but I thought he would have immediately noticed on his own. He had finished chewing and even taken a small swallow when I whispered to him that he had just eaten spackle.

"What?" he asked curtly.

After confirming what I had just said, my husband made an incessant lunge toward the bathroom. The sound of his heaving and spitting was quite enough to scare away the Chinese man waiting patiently to be called to the chair for a haircut. He slammed the door behind him as he left the shop in quite a hurry. Honestly, I was not as concerned with the loss of a customer as I was with the possibility of having poisoned my husband. As I called our doctor, newspaper headlines flashed through my mind:

LOCAL BARBER POISONS HUSBAND WITH SPACKLE SANDWICH

Or

LOCAL MAN SHITS BRICKS

At the time, it seemed very reasonable to me that headlines like these could soon monopolize the front page of the local newspaper. This is something I was not prepared for.

The doctor had good news, though. He said that spackle in that small a quantity was virtually harmless. He added that some good might come out of all of this after all. He suggested that if we were to save Gary's next stool sample, that we might possibly have the materials to be able to fix that hole in the ceiling after all.

Halloween Fun

I've always thought of Halloween as one of those holidays that magnify the personalities of the eccentric and strange. This being said, one need look no further than The Progressive Barber Shop for evidence of this philosophy.

Sue Kemp, a longtime friend, co-worker and Godmother to my youngest son happens to have been born on Halloween Day, which is appropriate because in my eyes, she is the personification of the spirit of Halloween. I think that this fact, as well as other factors, has had an impact on the way that our shop has approached the Halloween celebration over the years. Allow me to elaborate.

Every year, the girls and I dress up for Halloween. Occasionally, we have dressed appropriately considering we are a business that deals with all sorts of people from a wide variety of religious, political, and cultural backgrounds. As an example, a few years back I dressed in a brown robe, adorned with a hood and sash, and wore an empty bag of potato chips on my head. *What was I* you might be asking. I was a *chip* monk. Yes, albeit cheesy, but not without imagination and creativity; and never without careful thought.

There have been occasions, however, when the costumes that we have concocted were…let's say…morally questionable. Again, allow me to elaborate.

Last year, Linda and I decided that we were going to dress up like the nuns did in back in grammar school. We got our hands on genuine habits and wore oversized crucifixes around our necks. We looked very authentic, right down to the pregnancy suits we had beneath our robes. That's right, we went as pregnant nuns!

We had a day full of laughs within the confines of the barber shop; but, as one might expect, Linda was met with a certain degree of contempt when she waddled her way through the checkout line at a local gas station with an eighteen pack of Genny Light pinned under her arm. Hey, there is something to be said about keepin' it local, right?

This latter story is a true testament as to the nature of the shop's clientele and its employees. We continue to have a client base that spans anywhere from Orthodox Jews to high ranking city officials to parolees and everything in between. On any given day you might walk in to find the Mayor carousing with the local Rabbi, a local college sophomore discussing politics with a 90 year old woman wearing leather pants, or a construction worker arguing in high tones with a bum who has just exposed himself through the front door window.

With all this, you might think that there would be more outrage at some of our intra-shop antics, but really, there is not. Transcending all the tomfoolery, the gags, and the language (you cannot forget the language), there is a level of comfort, comradery, and equality in the shop that is almost extinct within today's society.

And although I will be the first to admit that the atmosphere in our shop is not always conducive to politeness, good manners, or political correctness, it consistently, *without fail* provides temporary relief from the pressures of the world outside. I like to think that my customers - my friends - understand this on some level. I suppose that is how I internalize their coming back week after week, month after month, year after year, decade after decade.

Linda and I as the pregnant nuns. Notice our stoic expressions and fisted hands!

Regina (the angel) and I as a chip monk (get it?) with a customer last year on Halloween.

Even our customers get into the Halloween spirit. Our good friend Rick came into the shop one year sporting his 'summer' teeth (some are here - some are there). All of us girls were stumbling over our words, none of us wanting to cut this creature's hair. We did not recognize him at first. When we learned the Hillbilly's true identity, he got a free haircut for the most realistic costume

Nice Coon Hound, Rick!

Don't Get Mad, Get Even

As my friend Rick has demonstrated so nicely in the preceding picture, some of my clients (and friends) occasionally get the best of their old friend, Pattie. One of my old friends, Jim, came into the shop one day and got a haircut. He did not realize until his haircut was finished that he had forgotten to get cash before coming in for his appointment. Our shop does not have an ATM and we do not take credit cards, so this kind of thing happens frequently.

Without hesitation, I let told Jim that I would accept a personal check, which he wrote gratefully. At the end of the day, I stuffed my earnings into my purse, as per usual, and hurried to the bank to make a deposit. As the bank teller was thumbing through my checks, she looked up at me with a curious look on her face, and embarrassment in her eyes. In her hand was Jim's 'personal' check.

I asked her if I could take a look at the check, and she handed it over. In the lower left-hand corner, Jim had written in perfect penmanship, "For Sexual Favors." I was so embarrassed. After all, what kind of sexual favors could I have possibly performed for a lousy fifteen dollars? Seriously, though, after turning five shades of red, I hurriedly finished my bank business and fled the scene. Jim had gotten me good, but as the saying goes – It ain't over 'till the fat lady sings. And I hadn't even started warming up my voice, yet.

As luck would have it my dear friend James accidentally left his wallet at my shop soon afterward. Being the Good Samaritan that I am, I called to tell him about it and told him to come down to pick it up. The next day he did just that. About two hours later the phone rings and Jim was on the other end bellowing laughter. He went to the bank and when asked by the teller to see his ID, he opened his wallet. Lying there across his driver's license was a finger condom. (A surgical rubber that you slide over your fingers for any number of reasons) It looks exactly like a miniature condom. Ironically his teller had the same look on her face as did mine. I don't know what was funnier, the rubber *or* the size of it! I guess you could say the fat lady had sung.

Double Exposure

Owning a barbershop in the city, everyday you meet new and exotic people. One summer afternoon, a street urchin came into the shop looking for a bargain haircut. He came in and asked if we would clipper his head for five dollars. There was no way! For one thing, we charge fifteen dollars for a haircut of any kind; and this is not to mention the fact that this guy looked as though he had spent the last ten years searching for sticky treasures in alleys and dumpsters across the city. He was dressed like a tramp and had parked his grocery cart in the alley next to the barber shop.

I told him I could not do it, but there was a place down the street that might be able to help him out. He refused to take no for an answer. Instead, he took a seat in the waiting area and continued to mumble at me from under his breath. Luckily, there was a customer there with me, as well as my youngest son. They both witnessed what happened next.

I hear my customer, who I am working on in my chair, frantically yell, "Sir, you need to leave…NOW!" He then instructed me to call 9-1-1 immediately. My son and I, both wondering what the matter was, looked up in time to see this man manipulating his man-piece. Sitting there, just playing with it in front of everyone!

I did not even have the 9 dialed when my son flew toward the man and forcefully, but carefully, escorted him to the curb outside, where he collapsed. I was not even sure that he had put his livestock back in the barn. Ouch!

The 9-1-1 operator gave a feeble effort to contain her amusement when I explained to her our situation. I told her to feel free to laugh; after all, all of us were hysterical by this time.

The cops came shortly after and took the nut away (no pun intended). Of course, it would not be the last we would see of him.

Raw Liver Tips

It's funny how strange things seem to happen in pairs. A few weeks after the hobo exposed his little friend to us, something else happened that changed me profoundly. I was in the middle of a haircut when Karen, a co – worker, went outside to have a cigarette. A few minutes later, the phone rings and its Karen on her cell. She was looking back at me through the front window yelling, "Did you see it? Look at the guy in the chair!" I glanced over only to see the man with his legs crossed, and his boys hanging out! Being an elderly man, his boys were hangin' low. I dry heaved.

What could I do? The boys were turning purple, so I had to do something quick. They looked like uncooked liver patties with straggles of patchy hair coming out of them. I promptly asked him if he would get me a cup of coffee. He got up and soon his pals went back home. The horror has stayed with me every day since. Raw liver tips – gross.

Don't Shoot the Messenger

Jan missed her calling. At the drop of a hat, she can and will bellow out a song that would blow your mind. She has a truly beautiful voice and loves to share it with all of us at the barber shop. Jan is our mail lady.

My customers have come to appreciate her taking requests and performing her songs into our makeshift microphone (a common push-broom handle). I can honestly say that I have never heard of another mail person who performs like mine; and, all the while doing her business without interruption.

For my birthday last March, Jan entered the shop singing *Happy Birthday* in front of a shop full of customers. It was so sweet. Her ovation was still chiming as she dropped off the mail and went on her way.

Kickin' it Olde School

Some of the most enjoyable experiences I have had in my professional career have been working with elderly gentlemen. My first visit to a retirement community came at the request of my children's pediatrician and my longtime friend, Dr. Decanq. The Doc asked me if I would go to his father's retirement home and give him a haircut. I was delighted to help! His dad's name was Ducky and he was a real sweetheart.

Before too long, I was being called regularly for other haircuts at the home. I remember this one old man that I would work on; his wife had told me that he was not responsive to his surroundings and I did not have to be too fussy with his hair because he would not know, anyway. Although he was all slumped over in his chair when I walked in, I soon came to realize how wrong his wife had been. I talked to him while cutting his hair. I told jokes and laughed. The whole time I was under the impression that he did not know I was there. As I started toward the door, ready to leave his room, I glanced back at him only to see his eyes open a tiny bit, and he gave me the most delicate and sweetest smile I've ever seen. He *did* know that I was there and although he could not vocalize his appreciation for my services, his smile was my thank you. Next time I went back to do his hair, he was gone. A nurse had told me that he had died.

In many ways, business mimics life. As people get older, heading into their golden years, the population of their peers inevitably becomes scarce. I see my father, now eighty-six years old, saddened by the loss of so many friends and family members who had all experienced parallel lives together. From my own experiences as a successful business owner, I have had the misfortune of seeing many clients and friends pass. It is truly a catch 22. Although longevity as a business owner suggests financial success, professional prowess and community support, it also brings with it the sadness of having to see old friends (and young friends) pass. But, just as is the case in life, these people, although unforgettable, are replaced by new clients, new friends, and new experiences. I look forward to meeting them all and sharing unique experiences together.

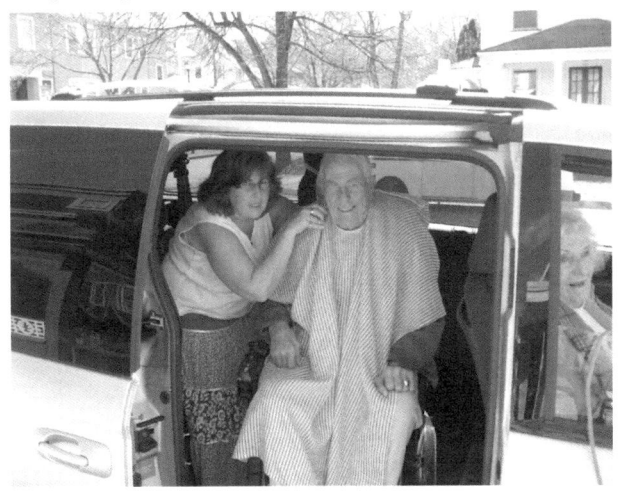

Me hunched over in Mr. Sherwood's van

Another elderly client of mine always pulls his van up to the curb in front of the barber shop, where I proceed to cut his hair - on the curb, and in the back of the van. He is wheelchair bound, so I feel it is my responsibility (and privilege) to help him. I run an extension cord from an outlet in the shop to his vehicle and work inside it, hunched over and cramped. After I finish his hair, I can't stand upright for the rest of the day. I always remember to wear sneakers and cut fast when I do Mr. Sherwood, or else I will surely pay for it the next day. Then there are the occasional clients that make you feel honored just to have the opportunity, no matter how brief, to interact with them. My shop is located across from a synagogue in a primarily Jewish community. Occasionally, I will get an elderly customer and will catch a glimpse of the numbers tattooed on his arms. Holocaust survivors have a way of putting everything into perspective. One of my favorite customers was a survivor. After every haircut, he would say, "God bless you and your family." I would never accept more than five dollars from this old man, whose name I never knew. The simple fact that he still believed in God after experiencing what he had experienced made his blessing that much more profound and meaningful to me.

The Candy Man

Mr. D. is the candy man. He is a long-time, loyal Progressive customer who, whenever he comes in to get his hair cut, brings with him a bag of candy. He is pushing ninety years old and has been coming to the Progressive Barber Shop since he was a little boy. He is a pleasure when he sits in the chair. He sings the most beautiful Jewish songs, he recites Shakespearean sonnets, and is always happy to lend advice laden with the wisdom

Sue and me with Mr. D.

of age. I always give him my undivided attention.

In addition to his intellect, Mr. D. has a unique sense of humor. He loves causing discomfort by talking to strangers about the leg he lost in World War II. He likes asking them which leg they think it might be. I've found that people never quite know how to respond to questions about prosthetic limbs being asked by strange old men. His stories of his dog mistaking his prosthetic leg for a chew toy are priceless.

Mr. D. dances, too! He has been known to spring up from the chair, mid-cut, and swing to the tune "Me and My Shadow." His rhythm is outstanding. If I was only fifty years younger, I probably still would not be able to keep up with old Mr. D.

He is the old man whose stories you never get tired of hearing because you never hear the same one twice and they are all exciting and entertaining. I look forward to hearing new ones every time we meet.

We Fix Eight Dollar Haircuts

Haircuts are a funny thing. Everybody needs them eventually; and some people need them more than others. I will be the first to admit that it can get expensive having to schedule a hair appointment every two, three, or even four weeks. At my barber shop especially, where we charge fifteen dollars for a man's haircut.

I assure you, however, that fifteen dollars seems a lot more reasonable when you consider all the $8.00 haircuts that my girls and I have had to fix over the years. Unfortunately for the customer, we still have to charge full price to fix a haircut that some other shop screwed up. In the end, you're paying $23.00 for a haircut that is just going to grow out in two weeks anyway. My belief is that people should just come and pay the extra money to have their haircuts done right the first time.

There was a point, in fact, where my girls were fixing so many botched haircuts from other commercial hair salons, that I actually had a friend of mine print T-shirts reading:

PROGRESSIVE BARBER SHOP, WE FIX $8.00 HAIRCUTS

Believe it or not, the shirts sold like hotcakes. It was kind of an awkward situation when we were

The Progressive Barber Shop parade float

asked to put a float in a local parade advertising our business, and we ended up being situated right behind a float advocating for one those $8.00 salons. We were all wearing our shirts, too!

My Pleasures

Although elderly people have given my girls and me much joy over the years, nothing can compare to the feeling of contributing to the happiness of child. Having two boys of my own, I have been blessed on more than one occasion to be able to do just that. Even if it is not me directly doing the deed, simply witnessing another person going out of their way to brighten up a child's life is remarkable.

It was about a year ago when one of my Doctor friends at Strong Memorial Hospital called to tell me about a young boy who had been diagnosed with an untreatable form of cancer. He had been receiving chemotherapy and was losing his hair. He wanted to have it all buzzed off to appear more normal looking. Karen had volunteered to go to the hospital to cut the little boy's hair.

A police officer in my chair had overheard the entire conversation and handed Karen a twenty dollar bill, requesting that she tell the little boy that it was a gift from the boys in blue. Karen came back to the shop, detailing how excited the boy was as a result of the gift by the anonymous policeman. She said that the boy had a million questions for her about the officer. Sadly, I heard that the little boy died a short time later; but

Karen, myself, and I am sure the officer felt a bit of joy knowing that this child, in the midst of all the sadness and fear that had no doubt consumed him, had his spirit lifted by the generosity and thoughtfulness of a caring stranger.

In case you're not sad enough already, having just read that last anecdote, here's another that will surely bring the waterworks:

A runaway twelve year old boy comes running into the shop one afternoon, disheveled and crying that he had lost his backpack running away from a group of bullies. The girls and I did our motherly duties and calmed him down, bought him lunch, and gave him a free haircut to take his mind off of his troubles (because that always works!). Again, a thoughtful customer in my chair, this time a fireman, handed the boy $5.00 and wished for him that he would have a better day.

We ended up getting his home phone number, and we called his mother. We learned that the boy had recently lost his father and he was understandably having a hard time coping with the loss. By the time his mother came to get him, he was smiling and he even said that that had been the best day of his life. I never saw them again, but his words melt my heart whenever I think about them.

Pat

One of the most cherished and memorable friendships I've had at the barber shop was with a very special man named Pat. Pat had been diagnosed with an inoperable brain tumor; and, as is so often the case with chemotherapy treatments, he had started to lose his hair. Linda and I convinced him to shave his head rather than to wait for his hair to fall out gradually. Being proactive in his decision–making, as opposed to letting the cancer dictate the rest of his life, really seemed to strengthen his resolve in living with such a terrible disease. He even began bragging to everyone that he should have done it years ago because women loved it. Pat's positive attitude, his sense of humor, and his overall personality really appealed to me. We became close friends.

Within weeks of his diagnosis, Pat was forced to retire from work. He had been an electrician for many years. Now without gainful employment, he began spending more time at the shop with us. I like to think that the company and atmosphere of the shop comforted him in some way during such a difficult time.

Knowing how much it upset him having to give up a job that he loved, I thought he might appreciate doing some work for me at the shop. As it worked out, the shop needed a good interior paint-job, anyway. I asked him if he might be interested. Just as I had anticipated, he jumped at the chance. I gave him a key so he could come and go and he pleased and work at his own pace. By the time he was finished, the shop looked wonderful. He really did do an outstanding job.

Sadly, within a couple of months, Pat lost his battle with his cancer. I made a promise to myself never to paint over his work. This was a promise intended to honor my friend, and it is a promise I have kept. I have since covered the walls of my shop with a mural of customers' pictures- hundreds of them- never disturbing the off-white layer of paint my friend had coated upon my walls. I think of Pat every time a new photo goes up.

Ironically, years later, as I glanced around at the countless pictures on the shop walls and considered all the memories that accompanied them, one picture I was missing was Pat's. Although this may seem sad at first, I was reassured knowing that Pat's handiwork served as a backbone to my wall of memories; and, his memory, although not captured in a photograph, resided in my mind just as vividly as any digital image could have provided.

Only this past Christmas did Bill, a mutual acquaintance of Pat and myself, provide me with a picture of my friend that now hangs proudly on my wall.

The wall that Pattie built---err…painted. Littered with photographs, Pat's handiwork can still be seen toward the bottom of this picture.

Is there a Doctor in the House?

Having such a diverse clientele does have its advantages. Although I am not completely sold on the effectiveness of flu shots, one particularly brutal flu season, I was persuaded to get one…albeit mostly out of convenience. Also, considering the sheer volume of people I come into contact with on a daily basis, I figured it might be the responsible thing to do, anyway.

I had been mulling over the idea for a while when one day the shop door opens and in walks my children's pediatrician, Doctor D.

Apparently, he had grown tired of hearing me talking about setting up an appointment because he walked over to me, rolled up my sleeve, took a syringe from a white envelope and stuck it in my arm-right there at the shop! Who says doctors no longer make house calls?

In a completely unrelated incident, one of my co-workers, Linda, had been complaining about a kink in her neck. As if on cue, in walks my physical therapist for an appointment (a haircut, I mean; not a therapy appointment). Anyway, soon after Linda was laid out on the floor as if in some medieval rack with Dr. Steve straddling her back, practically twisting her head off of her shoulders. He was yanking her so hard, that he was literally pulling her writhing body across the floor. I remember thinking this is what it must have looked like when the cavemen chose their mates.

In the middle of this whole ordeal, in walks a judge; nonchalantly, he comes in, steps over Linda and her assailant, sits in the chair and begins to read the newspaper. It was as if he had not even noticed her; as if she were not there at all! I lost it. I began bellowing at the absurdity of the whole situation. I laughed so hard, I peed. Anyway, Linda's neck did feel better, afterward. In the end, I decided we all needed doctors – head doctors!

Buzz Cuts

The Upper Monroe area in Rochester is a nice place to loiter on a warm summer day. Often times, between appointments, the girls and I hang out in front of the shop in lawn chairs. One day, Karen and I were out in front of the shop when the bartender from the restaurant came over with a tray and a pair of drinks. One of my customers had been indulging in a tasty beverage next door, saw us sitting outside and decided to buy us a round. I got a gin and tonic and Karen had gotten a mudslinger. And they were HUGE!

You can imagine how easily cold beverages went down on this steamy summer day. The second round went down just as easily! Unfortunately for us (and for our unsuspecting customers), we still had appointments to do that afternoon. I'll tell you what--- you know you're good when you're putting out acceptable haircuts with unsteady hands, slurred speech, and double vision. Actually, it was some of my finest work. Kind of the way that girl at the end of the bar is so fine just before last call.

On another occasion, the girls and I actually put a hand-written sign on the door, letting our customers know that we were next door having a few well-deserved, mid-afternoon drinks. A few of them actually joined us for cocktails! Five customers had decided that drinks took precedence over haircuts that particular day; and they ended up rescheduling.

I can only imagine what their wives were thinking when their husbands came home half-cocked and shaggier than when they had first left. We are supposed to be running a business, after all, not a bar tab.

P-hair Trade

The nice thing about being your own boss is being able to trade services with clients. Over the years, I have traded many things in exchange for free haircuts (not what you are probably thinking). I still remember the very first thing I traded for haircuts. I traded a full year of haircuts for the closing fees on my husband and my first house. It was a hell of a trade, and a very generous thing for my lawyer-friend to have done for us in a time when we were less than financially capable.

Make no mistake, however; I am not the only person who has benefited from trades like these (consider the price of a haircut these days is $15.00). One of my longtime friends and one of the best handymen in the city has benefited greatly from the combination of my being completely incapable of completing even the most menial home repair and my fortunate profession. He has replaced light fixtures for us, repaired our barber pole, and replaced sockets. He has done it all. On a few occasions, I even had him do some work on our home. He would come over in the mornings, and after a few Baileys and coffee, I would leave for work and he would complete the task I had given him. And he always did such a great job.

Recently I made a trade for one hundred dollars worth of food at Jeremiah's tavern with Greg, a photo trade with Jeff, a chair caning trade with Jim and a cathouse trade with James. That trade made some kitty very happy! 23 years ago, I made a trade with my friend Buzzy for several exotic cacti for my barber shop window. They were tiny when I first got them, but you have to see them now; they're huge! People marvel at them all the time. One of them stands about 6 feet tall and is about 4 feet in diameter!! They are really quite beautiful.

I have traded for many small favors with all sorts of people from a variety of different occupations. If you knew my kids, however, you would understand that some of the best trades I have made over the years have been with lawyers, policemen, and doctors.

Pain in the Glass

The way that the progressive Barber Shop is set up is unique. It has two large bay windows facing the Avenue, and if you are inside, looking out, there is a three paned glass door to the left of the big windows. Other than this, there are only two other attic-like windows in the entire place – one in the bathroom and one on the wall adjacent to the front door.

Having a street-front glass window has its advantages as well as its disadvantages. On one particularly sweltering Rochester summer afternoon, the entire block lost power, likely due to the overuse of air conditioning. Well, the windows at the shop face Westward, and in the afternoon, without an air conditioner, the shop can feel as uncomfortable as…well… it can feel like a soup can stuffed with burning hair, floating on a hot spring. Yes, it can be that unpleasant.

On top of the sheer discomfort of the whole thing, the girls and I had to finish out the day using the blazing sun as our only source of light; we had to use razors to clean up the necks of our customers after their haircuts, and we had to use scissors to finish any buzz cuts that had to be done. Believe me; using scissors to buzz someone's head is tougher than you might think. In the heat, Regina (the new addition to the shop) began to hyperventilate and went into the bathroom to open one of the two accessible windows in the shop, in hopes that it would create a cross breeze. In her haste, however, the window shattered and a million little pieces rained on her like white-hot diamonds.

At one time or another, every piece of glass in the shop has had to be replaced. One afternoon, around closing time, a customer of mine arrived to find the front door locked, and the sign read *CLOSED* as I was preparing to go home after a long day (of course I would stay and finish him, however). Fooling around, he began to pound his fists on the top pane of the door, and sure enough, it fell out and shattered all over the place. As it happened, we both ended up staying later than planned that night because we had to repair the window. He did get a great haircut on top of it all – a testament to my professionalism. There is no denying he is a madman, just as there is no denying that he is also my friend. This is the case with too many of my clients.

Per Capita, the crime rate in Rochester, New York is very high. I consider myself lucky because, for the most part, my business has not fallen victim to too much crime. That is not to say, however, that I have avoided crime completely. Several years ago, I received a telephone call from the Police stating that there was an incident at the shop. It was Easter Sunday.

As it turns out, a neighborhood kid that I had known since he was five years old had broken through the glass front door and burglarized the shop. He had stolen a few dollars that I had left in my drawer that night-something that I rarely did prior to this incident, and have never done again. The unfortunate thing is he broke in again a few weeks later, this time entering through the attic-like bathroom window. This time, he swiped a pair of clippers and a few brushes. I guess he wanted to look good when he went into jail, which is where he ended up as a result of his second breaking and entering at the Progressive Barber Shop. I still can't understand why he did not take the television, or a chair, or something worth more than a brush and a pair of clippers. Well, he now has 4-6 years to think about it.

Accidents will happen

Even though for more than thirty years, the girls and I have been so painstakingly careful and particular, and above all, responsible (as I am sure you will agree), accidents are inevitable. Most accidents, ironically enough, have had little to do with the copious amounts of glass that enclose the shop.

One busy day, while I was completely engulfed in the rhythm of the business, the weather changed. Drastically. Anyone who has lived in, or even visited upstate, New York during one of these miracles of nature will verify what I am telling you. The calm and hazy sun of the early afternoon exited with such haste that day, that there actually seemed to be a wake that came through the region afterward. The wind kicked so violently, that it actually detached our 10 foot by 3 foot sign from the front of our building. A *huge* sign, attached with cement screws and the strongest kind of fastening apparatuses. Thank the lord no one was walking by at the time.

About eighteen years ago, one of my customers came into the shop for an appointment with his one year old baby boy. We were all shootin' the breeze, and Dan hoisted his son onto his shoulders without a second thought. Both fans in the shop were on high. You can imagine our bewilderment when that little boy's forehead was filleted by the fan blade. Luckily, dad was alert and stopped the bleeding (oh, the bleeding) even before the ambulance arrived a *very* short time later. You can usually gage the severity of an injury by the reaction time of city paramedics. They were fast. The baby ended up receiving over twenty stitches, but healed and was fine.

This incident really affected me. Even hours later, after I had calmed down and finished the day at the shop, I had to pull my car over on the way home and vomit off of the interstate. After a good cry, I did everything I could to put that wretched day behind me. Thank God dad and his baby were going to be fine.

The Ice Capades

I am going to piggy back on theme of man vs. Rochester weather for a second. It was the first week of March, 1991 when we had the ice storm in Western New York. I strongly recommend you *Google* it if you were not there, or can't remember. Mother Nature was especially brutal that year. Some were without power for nearly three weeks. Every bush and tree in the area looked like it had been transformed into crystal. Amazingly enough, the shop did not lose power or heat even for a minute, and I did not miss even a day of work. As a matter of fact, business boomed. In addition to the customers that actually came in for haircuts, people came in for pizza, beer, and warmth, as well. I was so happy that I could help my fellow Rochestarians in some little way; plus, I earned a few extra bucks that helped pay for the firewood we used to heat our home. We were not so lucky at home, you see.

Rochester winter. Buffalo... Schmuffalo!

We were without power for 2 weeks. Even though mother nature was ruthless that year, you had to appreciate how pretty things were as a result of her doing. Gotta' love Rochester weather (or deal with it, anyway)!

Hot and Cold

On a 90 degree summer day, it's not good business practice to have your air conditioner bite the dust, especially when you work in an oven-sized brick building with very little ventilation. Not only is it rough on the barber, but it can be hell on the poor guy covered with the nylon cape, as well. Until you can resolve the problem, using fans are about the best thing you can do. Even then it becomes something of a tradeoff. Just imagine putting a stiff warm breeze on a wet face beneath a waterfall of flying hair. The hair sticks like glue. Plus, you have to constantly rewet the hair because damp hair tends not to blow around as much as dry hair, so the humidity gets progressively worse and worse. It's all you can do from passing out. The client ends up soaked to the gills and his eyes are burning from the sweat teeming off his brow. No amount of powder can help to relieve his sticky face. Then there are the poor fools who have crossed the fan's path: Werewolf-looking customers waiting for their turns to get tortured. The only saving grace is that everyone is in the same boat.

On the other hand, in the middle of a cold winter day, having your furnace clonk out can also be a problem. That's exactly what happened on this one particular day. The thermometer read about 50 degrees. The girls were wearing their coats while cutting hair and so were the customers while they sat in the chairs. At one point my hands started to go numb and I had a terrible time holding the scissors. I finally managed to get a hold of the landlord and told him that if we didn't get the heat on soon, we were all going to look like ice sculptors...or sculptures—either way, I guess. Shortly after that, he brought a space heater over to thaw us out and within a short time the furnace was fixed. What a chilling experience that turned out to be.

Prick

Recently, a fellow business owner called me up to see if I could house a few cacti that he was trying to get rid of. I already had several of them in my shop window and they do very well, so I said yes, and my husband and I went over to Gary's place to collect them. To my surprise, there were at least ten of them, of all types and sizes. Most cacti are not easy to move, and these were no exceptions. Loading them in the cars was a freaking nightmare! When we finally did get them to their new home, we had been pricked so many times; it looked as though we had been to an acupuncturist! We were pulling out tiny prickers for days.

Even the man who washed my shop windows refuses to do the inside of my windows for fear of getting impaled. He said that there is not enough money in the world to persuade him to get near those booby traps. When I water them, it looks like I've been the referee in a cat fight, with tigers. You might ask why I have them. I think that anything that pretty is worth a bit of pain. Besides, one day they could come in handy. They could prove to be the perfect weapon against some of the whacko's running around the Avenue. Beware, or I will prick you to death!

One afternoon Karen decided, against all odds, to water the cacti. After a few short minutes, I heard her scream, "Damn it! " When she turned around, her shirt was soaking wet on one side. She looked like she was lactating! When she bent over, one of the cacti pricked a hole in her water bra! She was leaking like a faucet. She was pissed. I tried to tell her that it could have been a lot worse … it could have pricked the real deal! Come to find out, she was mad mainly because Wal–Mart had discontinued selling the water bras. Talk about bad luck! What a boob. No pun intended!

The Wolves

Every day I am thankful for being able to work a job that I truly love. In addition to this fact I am also thankful, knowing that as long as there are people with hair, my services will always be needed. After all, everyone (besides Willie Nelson and Manny Ramirez) gets their hair cut. I have had Supreme Court Justices as clients, as well as doctors, lawyers, Mayors, teachers, CEO's of major local corporations, millionaires, and multi-multi millionaires.

One of my most memorable clients was actually 5 clients. They had been next door to the shop doing laundry, and came over to ask if they could use our phone to order a pizza. Obviously, this incident preceded the cell phone revolution. Anyway, the five little men ended up hanging out just like so many other clients and friends. They got their pizza, fiddled around with their hair and were quite sociable and friendly. Good people.

I would not even have known who they were if it wasn't for the young girls pressed up against the windows, looking in and screaming out for the men in my chairs. They were Los Lobos (The Wolves); the Latino band responsible for re-popularizing a little tune you might know called *La Bamba* for a movie by the same name in the early 80's! How cool is that?! It just goes to show that you never know who is going to walk through that door.

Sometimes it's Snot for Me

The combination of baby powder, 30 years worth of facial hair trimmings, dust, hairspray, gel, cologne and about one hundred other things can sometimes agitate the sinuses. On one particular occasion, there was a gentleman in my chair, and he began to have one of those dreaded sneezing attacks; one after another, after another. When he finally stopped, I resumed with his hair cut. About halfway through, I looked down and saw a mucus green glob of jelly trembling on the man's forearm. A nose slug; a snot rocket. I began to dry heave.

I did not have the heart, or the stomach, to let the man in on the secret that only I knew. I finished the man's haircut as fast as I could. It took all I had in me not to evacuate all that was actually inside of me. He left that day, but even now, when the same guy comes in to get his haircut, I still cringe at the memory of the green jelly on his arm. Sorry guys, but the identity of this man I cannot reveal.

It's a Man's World

All men are similar, and for the most part, I try to believe that most men are good. Looking back on my career, I can't help but think that the 1970's and 80's were times when the less desirable aspects of the personalities of men were magnified. In short, when I was younger, men were asses. Hmm, I wonder if there is any correlation between the behaviors of male clients and my age. Anyway, the whole manicuring process provides a perfect platform for jerky behaviors. A manicure demands that you are very close to the client, sometimes bent down so as to manipulate the hand. There would be a manicuring dish, filled with hot water, acting like a curtain, concealing all kinds of inappropriate touching and fondling by clients.

I recall there being this one guy-fat, ugly, rich, and twice my age-who use to get his kicks from grabbing my knees beneath the manicuring tray. When I told my boss about it, he would insist that the old pervert was harmless, and ask how much he had left me for a tip. It was usually a lot. Call me seasoned or call me older and more rigid, but if that were to happen today, the old man would get one warning before I castrated him.

Something else happened more recently that I still have a hard time accepting. There once was this guy named Mouse who had been a long-time customer of the shop, and who was a personal friend of mine. I remember him well. He was a local cab driver who always had foul smelling breath and wore undersized cap. One day, Mouse must have gotten into the arsenic, because he approached me from behind and aggressively cupped my fun-bags. Oh, the rage that must have filled my eyes as I spun around and threatened to kick the snot out of him. I have since heard that Mouse has been locked away, the dirty rat.

Men – O – Pause

What an interesting word for a woman's curse. When you run a barber shop with all women, it's a word to be reckoned with; especially considering the lack of estrogen creates a very realistic possibility of a mass murder! It's ten degrees outside and the door and windows are open; it's 90 degrees inside and the heat is on full blast.

"Are you girl's nuts!" is a common question in our barber shop. The sixty four thousand dollar question should be, "Why do they call it menopause?" Should not the men suffer as well? We women have been cursed beyond the realm of reasonable limits! We have periods and men-strual cramps for the better part of our lives, we get pregnant for nine long months, and we look like elephants for months after we deliver. Then some of us repeat the whole cycle again and again! Apparently, we're gluttons for punishment.

Eventually, we meet Mr. Men-o-pause. And what does a man contribute but five minutes of moderate sexual pleasure! So, please, if we want the damn barber shop door and windows open, grin and bear it. It's a small price to pay for a good haircut.

I recall the year 1975, when I learned that Gary and I were about to become first time parents. It was an exciting time and we were both bursting at the seams with pride. As the months went by, I progressively (get it?) blew up. I was only beginning my third trimester and already looked like I was 8 months along. Standing on my feet all day cutting hair was beginning to be a real task. By the time I actually reached 8 months, I could literally rest my scissors, edgers, and clippers on my belly - all at once – beside my lunch!

I had to give up shaves and facials because I couldn't bend over even a little without risking falling over. If I did fall, I wouldn't be able to get up without a crane and a harness. I had gained a whopping 52 pounds! Finally in my last month of pregnancy, I decided that if I couldn't reach my clients anymore, then it was time to hang up my scissors. So I did.

Quite frankly, the guys were breathing a little easier, too. The very next day Gary and I had a beautiful baby boy. We named him Gabriel David Parker. He had a full, thick head of black hair. He must have known mom was a barber. What a great day that was!

On a side note, when our second son Nathaniel came along, I had a little more sense than to work so close to his birthday. I took maternity leave at least half a week before delivery.

His First Shiner

As this last anecdote might suggest, there is, engrained within my family, an unrivaled work ethic. My son Nathaniel exemplified this perfectly when, at eleven years old, he took a job shining shoes in the barber shop. He decided to clean the dust off of old Mr. Sam's shine box, and put it to use after all these years of retirement. I bought polishes, rags, brushes, and anything else Nathaniel needed to start his first job. He even advertised in my window, creating a sign that read:

Shoe Shines Only 2.00

Even now, seventeen years later, I still have that old, faded piece of plywood.

Although business was a little slow that first week, Nathaniel soon had more work than he could handle. After all, even in 1991, two dollars was a bargain for a shine. I also attribute his success to his outgoing nature, which he naturally gets from his mother. Anyway, I still remember the very first tip he ever got. He was beaming. He thought he was rich; and at eleven years old, I guess, in a way, he was. With the amount of time it took him to do the guy's shoes, he should have tipped the customer! But the business was off the ground.

Another man, a Rochester City Policeman, came in a short time afterward, and dropped off what seemed like a closet full of shoes for Nathaniel to shine. The boy was thrilled nearly to death. His eyes turned into silver dollars, he began to stutter and shake, and his hair turned money green! Okay, maybe this is a slight exaggeration, but he was understandably psyched. The gentleman told him he would be back later that day to collect his shoes and to pay him for the work. Nathaniel got started right away.

Nathaniel did a consistently good shine, so where I once watched him closely, I now pretty much did my own thing, and let him do his own. Remember how I explained how a zealous work ethic runs in the family; well, so does colorblindness. Had I remembered this fact, I would have paid closer attention to my son's work. But the damage was already done. Brown shoes were blackened, and black shoes were shined with brown shoe polish. I stopped him as soon as I noticed, and after I finished the haircut I was working on, we both worked feverously to remove the wrong colored polishes. He was so embarrassed.

From that point on, it was our deal that Nathaniel matches the shoe to the polish and gets some form of clearance from a second party before starting each new shine. He was happy to oblige. By the end of that summer, Nathaniel had earned more than 100.00! Not bad for an eleven year old shine boy with bad eyes. He did learn an invaluable lesson as a result of the whole fiasco, however. Buy cheap polish - it comes off easier.

You Be the Judge

As is the case with any project that you dedicate significant sums of time to, certain milestones are to be celebrated. My thirty year anniversary of owning the shop was just such an occasion.

The date was October 5, 2003. The girls and I had compiled an impressive array of beer, booze, and food. So many customers, both recent and past, came to congratulate me on my being one of the oldest small businesses in Rochester. People brought us gifts, and my husband bought me the most beautiful arrangement of flowers. Everything was perfect.

There was one regret I had at the time, however. Nick Valentino, the man I had purchased the shop from so many years ago, and a man who I considered to be a true friend, had passed away the previous year. It saddened me not having him there to celebrate with me. If it were not for him, I would not have had such wonderful opportunities professionally and in life, in general.

In the middle of our celebration, I glanced out across the avenue, and saw a familiar-looking man heading toward the shop. The man came walking in the door, and his identity could not be mistaken. It was Nick's son, Joe Valentino. What a huge compliment. Joe, a Supreme Court Judge, had take time out of his, no-doubt, busy day to come in and celebrate with my friends, family, and Me. This honor meant more to me than Joe would ever know, and through his hug, I felt Nick's congratulations, as well. What a perfect topper to an already wonderful day. Thank you Judge Joe, and thanks to Nick, too! Good people.

Pattie Parker, owner of Progressive Barber Shop, gets a congratulatory hug from Justice Joseph Valentino on her 30 years in the business. Parker bought the shop from Valentino's father. Looking on is customer Bill Gilligan.

Hugging Judge Joe, with friend Bill, sitting

Hair's to the Kids

A few years ago, the girls and I decided to have a fund raiser for the kids at the Hillside Children's Center, a facility where children with a variety of problems live while they receive education and treatment. They also have a foster program if anyone out there would like to provide a good environment for struggling, but good kids. At the shop, we have come to know several of the Hillside kids and counselors, so having a cut-a-thon was something we wanted to do to help them out. Again, we provided ample food and drink, and half of everything we made went towards the Hillside Center.

I had an advertisement in the window, asking people to come on in and contribute to the cause, and they did. Many people came in just to donate money, not even needing haircuts. This was just another instance where Rochestarians selflessly came out to donate to and support a good and worthy local cause.

By the end of the day, we ended up raising $500.00 for the cause. A few of the Hillside kids even walked down to the shop for food and drink, and gave us a big thanks to boot. To us, this was a bigger payoff than the money we had worked to raise. Good job, girls!

Ironically, that night was the night when my shop was burglarized, as I have already explained about. The money that was stolen was the money that we had spent all day collecting for the kids at Hillside. Thank God for insurance, no matter how outrageous the premiums are.

It's a Learning Experience

When starting a new job, the pressures brought on by that first client can be crippling. I'll remind you that I, too, flunked the barbering test the first time I took it. Remember? Karen must have felt tremendous pressure during one of her first haircuts at the shop. She did, in fact, give a haircut from hell. I swear the Devil must have made her do it.

The client was a little old lady, brought to the shop by her female caretaker, for what was supposed to be a traditional fade haircut. I told Karen to do it because fades are usually the easiest types of cuts. Or so I thought.

By the time the haircut was finished, the lady looked like she was preparing to enter camp…at Auschwitz. There wasn't any hair left, really. Just fuzz. The lady resembled a well used tennis ball. Thank goodness senility had begun to set in as a result if the old lady's age, because she did not seem to fully understand what had just happened to her. Her aide didn't seem to be all that upset, either. She did comment, however, that it would be a while before Rose would need another haircut. We like positive thinkers!

When they left, Karen began to hyperventilate. She must have felt terrible for what she had just done to the old lady's head. I proceeded to try to calm her nerves and assured her that her technique, as well as her confidence, would improve with time. And it did. Karen was putting out top-notch haircuts only a short time later.

Are you Board Waiting?

A doctor friend of mine, who has been a loyal customer of over 30 years, comes in early sometimes for his appointments. He finds that playing with our appointment chalkboard relaxes him. The board hangs, unused, in the shop solely because it was one of the original pieces of décor from back in the 1920's. The Progressive Barber Shop was, in fact, the first shop in the city to operate primarily by appointment. The board is not used anymore because we find it easier and more convenient to use a modern appointment book instead.

Anyway, my friend loves to fill in the time slots with crazy, goofy names, both real and made up. He looks like a little kid in a candy shop, giggling to himself as he fills in the morning time slots with appointments for Tom Arnold, Tom Thumb, and Thumbelina. It's quite comical to see a grown man have such fun with a piece of chalk and a slab of slate. Hey, if I can contribute to helping an overly stressed doctor relax for a bit, then buying chalk is a small price to pay. Some of those names have stayed on that board for months and months, for if *anyone* changes *any* of his thought up names he has sworn to hunt them down and make them pay! You have to believe him; he's a doctor, after all.

Peek-a-Poo

Sometimes, when life seems too demanding; and work is strenuous; and the kids and the husband are being difficult; it helps to let my hair down (more so than usual). Usually, friendly pranks on my old friend Linda are the perfect remedies to my life-stressors. Laughter is good medicine, especially when it is at the expense of an old Hippie.

This one day, the girls were all very busy doing hair. The sitting chairs were full of clients. Linda had to excuse herself to go to the restroom. That is when Sue and I got the bright idea to pull a prank on 'ole Linda. We told the customers to wait a few minutes while we left the shop, then we sneaked around the building into the alley, and stood on our tippy toes, just barely able to peer in through the attic-like bathroom window.

Linda was sitting on the toilet, uhh… relaxing and looking around, when she happened to look up at the window and spotted two back alley peeping Toms watching her on the potty, doing her business. Sick, I know. All of a sudden, Linda let out a piercing scream, calling Sue and I bitches among a variety of other creative adult superlatives! The next thing you heard were the guys laughing and clapping their hands like the final act in Hamlet had just ended! For a grown, mature woman, Linda certainly has quite the *potty* mouth (pun intended).

Give me your Pesos

It was right before closing time when Tony, a good friend of mine, came in for a haircut. He had just gotten back from a vacation in Mexico and still had about 2,000 pesos in his wallet. When he was ready to pay me, he gave me the choice between the pesos and the cash. Of course, always looking for a deal, I chose the pesos. Two thousand seemed like a lot of loot to me. It had to be more than the price of a haircut; or, at the very least, equal to one. I couldn't wait to call the bank and find out how much money it was! Well, guess what? I got what I deserved. The stupid pesos were worth about 4 cents in U.S. currency. I will admit he got me on that one. And after a good laugh, he was a gentleman and made good on the haircut. But Tony, as dear a friend as you are, beware. I will get even. Como se dice revenge?

Twin City

Two of my favorite customers are a set of twins who live off of the avenue. Their names are Mary and Carol Ann. They live a block away from the shop and are two of the sweetest ladies I've had the pleasure of meeting. I call them the neighborhood watch dogs. They are aware of all the goings on, both good and bad, which happen in the neighborhood. They inform me of things I otherwise would not hear. I swear they must never sleep. They rescue animals in distress and help anyone in need. Neither has been married, but no matter, they are committed to caring for one another. They are as sweet as honey.

But don't piss them off. They are notorious for having silver tongues, perfectly capable of putting one in their place if absolutely necessary. One of them smokes and the other does not. One is quite thin while the other thinks she is fat. It isn't true. They both have the same haircut and come at the same time to have it done. They always have a cup of coffee after their haircut and hang around for a while to chat. They always stop at the local deli on their way home to buy rub off lottery tickets. When they first call for an appointment, I always pick them up and bring them to the shop, even though they walk home. Indeed, these two sisters are an asset to my business and the whole neighborhood. I look forward to their monthly hair appointment and sharing a cup of coffee and a donut with them.

I mention the twins because they are the personification of the entire neighborhood; the entire city. They are polite and caring, yet completely independent and strong. They are similar in so many ways and yet opposite in so many more. They are the embodiment of us all, and they are completely true. And it is for that reason they deserve their own chapter in a book rooted around Rochester culture.

Home Away from Home

Through the years, the barber shop has become a popular hangout for many of our local customers. Certain ones have retired, so they come more frequently. They might stop in for a cup of coffee or sometimes they just stop in to read the newspaper or to help me with the daily crossword puzzles. It is not uncommon that their stays exceed two or three hour chunks of time. It is a lot like *Cheers*. There are regular *bar*ber shop groupies with the same kinds of familiar faces and unique personalities.

Clay is one of these friends. He often falls asleep in the waiting chairs while watching morning television programs (*The Price is Right* or *The View*). Some of his naps have lasted up to and beyond a half hour. He's our Woody. Then there is Jan, our mail lady. She waltzes in, raids the candy jar, goes potty, then if we are lucky enough, she'll grace us with a song. She is our Cliff Claven. Our buddy Joe comes in for coffee, gets a mustache trim, and tells us his latest jokes. Then, off to work he goes. His stays are relatively brief, so I see him as more of a Frasieresque character. Let us not forget our pal Jim. He bounces in the shop, trims his own mustache and beard, and then goes next door to the bar to have a cold one. I can almost hear the chants as he walks through the pub doors:

"Norm."

Sheldon once offered to vacuum the shop floor because I had been too busy to finish it myself. I'll bet his wife Betsy would have loved to witness that. I love how my customers and friends feel so comfortable at my shop. It's a nice compliment to me as well as my friends, having created such a unique and friendly atmosphere together.

Shel, helping out.

The coffee is always here, boys! And even if you don't like my brew, feel free to throw a pot on yourself, and stay a while so we can finish it together.

Give Me a Jingle

About ten years ago, I began getting these weird phone calls at work. At first it was just someone breathing heavy on the line, but without words. As time went on, this person began to get progressively more verbal and vulgar. When the voice began threatening me, I called the phone company and they put a tap on the phone in order to trace the calls. I was so concerned; I even filed a police report. Being the go-getter that I am, I also began tape recording the calls.

A few weeks later, we found out that it was a teenager who lived a few blocks away who had been doing it. Where were the parents, you might ask. It turns out his parents were both hearing impaired and had no clue what he was up to. The cops went to the kid's house to talk to him with the parents. His mom and dad made him call me and the girls at the shop and apologize. He explained that he was just doing it for kicks and that he was sorry. At the time, I figured that the embarrassment of getting caught was punishment enough for the kid, so I did not press charges against him.

They say that the biggest contributor to adolescent delinquency is parents' unawareness. This was a great example of how true that is. Knowing my own kids as I do, I am sure that they were up to some of the same kinds of behaviors when they were younger. I am just thankful that the victims of my kids' teenaged antics were not as creative as their own mother when it came to tracking out their own pests (with few exceptions, of course). Kids will be kids, I guess. Numbskulls.

What's My Name, Fool?

When you have worked with so many people over such a long a period of time, it can be difficult to distinguish people by just their first names. Often times, with popular names like Bob, Tom, and Jim, I assign nicknames so that I can better discern one from another. Some of these names I use solely for myself, while others, I actually use when I talk to the customers. Some special customers actually answer to the nicknames I have given them, and identify themselves using their nicknames when scheduling appointments over the phone.

Weird Bob is a good example. Years ago, when I first met Bob, he came off as a little odd. You know those people; the ones who don't actually do anything to make them seem out of their heads, but you just feel that way for no particular reason. Well Bob is Weird, hence, Weird Bob (not to be confused with Bob Weir of the Grateful Dead).

Booze Bob is another fine example. Whenever I speak of the infamous Booze Bob, people automatically picture Otis, from Andy Griffith. The fact is Booze Bob is not an alcoholic, but a liquor representative for a major booze distributor. The name fits him so well; I have even heard his buddies refer to him by this clever moniker.

It would be a travesty if I didn't mention Frolicking Jim. Jim showed up for an appointment one day in an exceptionally good mood. When his haircut was finished, he paid me and skipped out the door. He looked like a little kid with candy. My husband has tried to imitate Jim's gait, but nobody can dethrone Frolicking Jim in the frolicking department.

There is also crazy Wally, a.k.a. Walnutto, Franfurger, Cobbs Hill Phil, Candyman Frank, Georgie Porgie, Pattie Cake, Richie Rich, and Skip-to-my-Lou. Of course, over the years, customers have also assigned me with fitting nicknames; but, this is supposed to be a family book, so I am not at liberty to repeat *those* names.

Pay No Attention to the Man behind the Curtain

Dianne, a dear old friend of ours, came with her husband to visit us one summer all the way from Arizona. Dianne and I have been friends ever since she used to work for me at the shop more than twenty years ago. She came into the shop one day, and we started reminiscing about all the crazy stuff we used to do together back in the old days. The customer in my chair just sat back, listened, and seemed to enjoy our stories.

Among other topics, we started talking about smoking marijuana (in the past, of course). We talked about good pot, bad pot, people we used to buy from, and things we used to do when we were ripped. Dan, Dianne's husband, raved about how it felt to get high and kayak down the Potomac River. I have to admit, that does sound fun.

When I finished my client's haircut, I pulled off his cape. Much to the surprise of my friends, my customer stood proudly, dressed in blue, gun, badge, cap, and all. He was a Rochester Policeman. The silence that followed was hilarious. I had known the entire time, but it took Dan somewhat by surprise. I can only surmise that somewhere along the line, the ol' stoners had had negative experiences with lawmen. Let that be a lesson to him: always be aware of who is listening?

I'm Feeling a Little Flushed

Unfortunately for everyone, my shop is so small that the bathroom is situated only a few feet from our work area. The girls and I are very aware of the possibility that someone could hear a plop, toot, or the trickle sound of pee hitting the bowl during a restroom visit. We have become masters of camouflaging it; be it by running tap water or by flushing the toilet before the job is finished. Guys, however, are different. Guys will pee like race horses, unleash thunder farts, and stink up the bathroom so badly that the paint peels off the walls…and think nothing of it! Forget men being from Mars and women being from Venus. It is differences in restroom behaviors that truly separate the sexes.

People will often stop in a store to use the bathroom. Even though my bathroom is the worst in the neighborhood, I permitted it for a while. That is until one weirdo ruined it for everyone. This kind of grubby looking guy started using my bathroom so often that I thought he was planning on making it his permanent address. He would stay in that little 4' by 5' room for upwards of a half hour at a time. I remember thinking this guy must either be ready to bust a kidney or have a severe case of constipation to sit on a toilet for that long. This one Saturday Linda called me at home to tell me that this guy was in the john for almost forty minutes and that she was really getting nervous as to what he might be doing in there. For all we knew, he could have died or been making a bomb in there!

I told her to give him five more minutes and if he still didn't come out or answer her, call the cops. Well, finally he opened the door, leaving without as much as a word. When the girls inspected the facilities after, they found it immaculate! Apparently after he had hand bathed himself, he cleaned up his mess. The next week he showed up again. But by this time I had posted a sign stating that only paying customers were allowed to use our facilities. When he found this out, he went berserk, calling me every fowl name in the book. He slammed the door, and down the street he went, cursing me all the while. Good riddance. Let someone else put up with his crap. No pun intended.

On a related topic, there is flatulence. It is not realistic to blame it on the dog when it is just you and the customer in the chair. There are techniques effective in disguising the lingering effects of flatulence that only the Master Barber knows. Step 1: Keep em' talking. It's a lot harder to identify gas when you're engaged in exhilarating conversation. Step 2: Baby powder the neck. That sweet smelling stuff has gotten me out of quite a few jams in the past. If the customer asks why you are burying his neck in powder, tell him that it help to remove lose hair. From time to time, however, no amount of baby powder and no conversation can undo what has been done. But that is okay. It was a great man who once said, "To *air* is human, and to forgive is divine."

Most Wanted

As I have stated before, for such a modestly sized city, Rochester has a relatively high crime rate. One week some time ago, all the local news stations had put out a bulletin, raising public awareness of a wanted criminal. An artist sketch was plastered all over the television, on flyers, as well as on billboards. It was impossible not to have the image of this wanted man etched in our minds.

One morning, arriving at the shop late (as usual), I came in and Sue was already busy with a client. The manhunt for the aforementioned criminal had been going on for almost a week by this point. I did a double take as I entered the shop that morning because the person in Sue's chair was a dead ringer to the man who had been on the highway billboards. What would you do in this situation?

I left.

No, no…please don't think I bailed on my friend Sue, leaving her with Rochester's most wanted criminal. I did not think that alerting Sue in the middle of a haircut would be the best way to deal with the situation. Who knows how one will react to such horrifying news? No scenario that I could have imagined would have turned out well had I alerted Sue right then. I b-lined it to the nearest phone booth and immediately called the police. Then I called Sue to inform her of me suspicion, and to tell her that the cops were on the way. I'm sure this put her right at ease (yeah, right). Panic, I am sure, began to set in.

As it turns out, it was all a false alarm. The guy turned out to be harmless. I'll be darned if he did not look like the drawing on television. I don't recall that gentleman ever coming back in for another haircut. I can't understand why, though.

Sue was a mess after the incident. Needless to say, she had some choice words for me when I came back into the shop. I just feel sorry for her next customer. Having your hair cut by a panicky, menopausal barber with sharp instruments is a danger I never want to have to face.

May I Help You?

Every few months one of the local barber schools will call and ask permission to bring their students down to my shop to observe and ask questions about running a business. They do this in order to teach first-hand what to expect when they graduate and go out on their own, either working in someone else's shop or running a shop of their own. I enjoy visits from the students because they seem to really like appreciate the opportunity to come by. They always seem very interested and I think it provides added incentive for them to finish school and get into the business.

Going to school is one thing; working in a real barber shop is another. Only when you are working can you really start learning the trade. Experience *is* the best teacher. Cutting hair, after all, is only a small percentage of the business. Learning how to socialize and communicate with all types of people is every bit as important. If you cannot do that, this business is not for you. How many regular customers do you think one could acquire if they had the personality of a water bottle? It would not be worth it if I were a paying customer to come in and be bored for a half hour every two weeks, no matter how good the haircuts were

The time you spend at the barber shop should be relaxing. It should be entertaining. Have a cup of coffee. You can have a beer if there are any in my fridge! My goal is to provide my clientele with more than just a good haircut (actually, a *GREAT* haircut). I try to provide solace and relief from the drabness of the day to day routine. If at the end of the day, I have accomplished this feat, then my own aching feet, sore back, and long hours are a small price to pay.

Of course I am aware that at the end of the day, it is still a barber shop. Fifteen minutes inside *Progressive* is not always enough to placate all of life's problems. I was reminded of this one unfortunate afternoon as a few gentlemen who had been at the bar next door came in to have their hair cut.

Somehow, the men's conversation had focused on a very recent tragedy involving a young local man. One of gentlemen said that the information being presented must have been wrong because the man they were speaking of was a good friend of his. In fact, they were best friends and had been together the previous night.

The men turned the shop television onto the local new channel, and sure enough, his best friend had passed away the night before. He had not known until that very moment. Inconsolably, he began sobbing. What were any of us to do but tell him how sorry we were for him? As wonderful an environment as the shop has, in a situation like this, a church seems a more appropriate place to grieve.

Mirror, Mirror on the Wall

It is inevitable that the girls or I occasionally get some guy in the chair who acts like a dick. Usually when this happens, we proceed to make obscene gestures behind the client's back and then wink at each other thinking that we are slicksters. For some reason this behavior makes us feel better about having to service jackasses.

On one occasion, I happened to land one of these idiots in my chair. He was rude, arrogant, and basically a total tool to me. Like a child, I was making faces and silently mimicking him behind his back. I have to admit I also made a few nasty hand gestures toward him, as well. As I glanced over at Linda, I could not help but notice her giving me this piercing look, obviously attempting to relay something to me without speaking. It turns out, Linda was trying to tell me how hard it is to mock somebody behind their back in a room full of mirrors! Had she used her words, she would have said, "Hey stupid, you're so caught."

My first instinct was to laugh, but I didn't dare. Not only would I have not been able to compose myself but I had not yet gotten paid, either. I quickly finished the haircut, and he did pay me, although he tipped me nothing and not surprisingly, never returned. It was then that Linda and I went into hysterics! Oh well, he should have been more courteous, and I should have been more careful. Lesson learned, however: when mocking an asshole, find the blind spot in their rear view mirrors.

Of Mice and Men

You might think that grown men have some idea on how they would like their hair to be cut. It is surprising how often this is not the case. This one guy comes into shop and pulls out a handwritten note from his wife. It contains precise instructions on how she wants her husband's hair cut. She even draws a sketch to make sure we understand it. I read the note, look at him and ask why mommy didn't pin it to his sleeve! Needless to say, he didn't find my comment humorous. It must have been my delivery.

This was also the man who was crawling under my sitting chairs on his hands and knees, trying to coax his three year old son into putting his coat on so they could go home. The kid was totally ignoring him, looking the other way and probably thinking what a puss his daddy was. I wonder what all his Dr. Spock books say about completely insubordinate children. Call me old fashioned, but I know how I would have handled my sons if they ever behaved like that, which they rarely, if ever, did. Well, until they got older, anyway.

I remember a time when another client came into the shop with his four year old son. He told me that he and his wife were on their third sofa because his little boy kept destroying them. He'd stain them, rip them, and cut them intentionally, just to ruin them. When I asked him how he disciplined the child, he did not have much to say. He and his wife didn't believe in spanking, a sentiment that has become all too popular these days. Meanwhile, Little Satan was slamming the door to my ice box like a drunken Hercules. I asked him several times to stop but he wouldn't take his evil little hand off the cooler's handle. Finally, I had it.

I should preface what happened next by saying that it is not common practice for me to discipline other people's children. In this case, however, it was my property that was being compromised by the little monster. I put my scissors down (I was in the middle of cutting dad's hair), walked over to the spoiled brat and began literally pulling and yanking him away from the cooler. After what seemed like at least a round or two, Dad stood up, grabbed the boy, and flopped him in the chair telling him to "stay," much like you would talk to a disobedient puppy. Not surprisingly, that was the last time I ever saw the two of them. Tragic that this was the outcome of yet another situation, but come on! Handle your children, people!

C-hair-ity

Are you one of those people who always seems to receive clothing for Christmas, birthdays, Mother's Day, Flag Day, Thursdays, and just about every other occasion over the course of the year. If you are anything like me, most of these gifts are too small, too big, too granny-ish, uncomfortable, or just plain hideous. For some reason, however, it's hard to simply throw them away, and with gas prices the way they are, it's too damn costly to drive to the mall and take them back. So what do you do?

I bag em' up and bring them to the barber shop! A free bag of clothes on the street is a more popular commodity than the Steak and Cheese Bagel Meal at *McDonalds*. You cannot just put a bag of clothes right out there in front of your store and expect someone to pick them up. Even homeless folks have some semblance of pride. In order to make these bags of hand-me-downs accessible to the 'consumers,' you must place them around the corner from the shop; either in the alley or behind the parking lot. This way, taking a bag of someone else's clothing is less conspicuous.

I have done this for years. Basically in the end, it cuts out the middle man that there would be if I were to donate to *The Salvation Army* or to *Goodwill*. And believe it or not, I have as dedicated clientele for my second-hand clothes as I do for my barbershop, albeit not as large. I have even had people come into the shop and ask me when the next shipment would be coming in; or *going out*, as the case may be. I see people walking on the Avenue with my clothes on all the time. Once, a lady actually approached me and thanked me for the pants she had been wearing. Funny thing is they were a pair of pants my husband drove himself nuts trying to find. He never did.

Let's just hope my husband doesn't see any of his clothes walking down the street one day, especially that ugly red shirt he said he loved so much!

The Scar's the Limit

Owning a business where you come into contact with new people on a daily basis, it is important to be able to find interesting topics to discuss. Initiating enthralling conversation, after all, is the best way to insure that a customer will return. I have found the perfect way to pry even the most timid turtles from their shells.

One of my customers came into the shop one day and started telling me the most interesting and horrifying story about one of his neighbors. It is not what you might think, however. It was not a story about the neighbor who parties loudly late into the night, or even about an embarrassing episode involving neighbor nudity. No. This gentleman's neighbor shot him twice; once in the stomach, and once in the neck. I can only speculate as to what would make a person do such a thing, but something tells me it was not about using the lawnmower too early in the morning. Thankfully, my customer who was a good friend, survived this ordeal.

Anyway, after telling the story, he takes off his shirt right there in the shop and showed me all three of his battle scars. In case you have noticed the discrepancy between the number of scars and the number of times I said he was shot, I can explain. The bullet that entered the man's stomach actually exited his body through his back, hence the *third scar!*

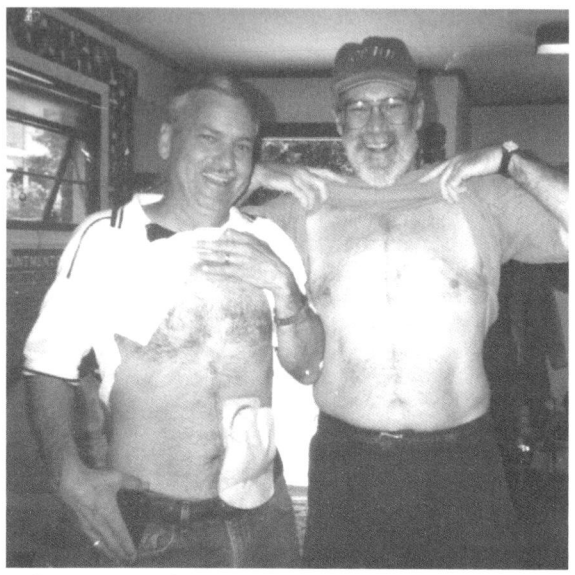

See my scar? I've got bigger ones than you!

How 'bout our's?!

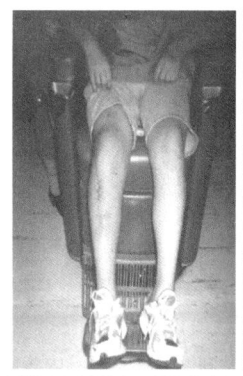

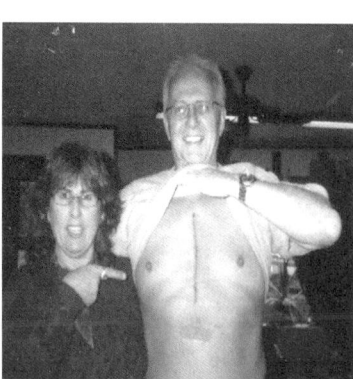

You would be completely shocked knowing how effective a photograph of a scar can be when trying to strike up conversations with perfect strangers. People see other people's scars, and without fail, they must share their own stories; or, at least a story of a guy they knew in college, or on a job somewhere.

I've since had guys share with me their scars resulting from open heart surgery; and one guy even begged me to put up a picture of him after he had gotten the short end of a nasty bar fight with some local thugs.

This is my remedy for having nothing to talk about with new customers. Since I hung that first picture of that poor man's bullet wounds, countless men, women, and children have offered to have their scars documented and shared, as well. One of the walls in my shop closely resembles an autopsy portfolio. Creepy, I know.

If I were to offer a bit of advice to the lefty liberals and the right-wing conservatives who can never seem to find any common ground, it would be to continue their conversations in my barbershop, because believe you me, a disturbing photograph of a caesarian section gone wrong or a badly burned nether region is a universal conversation starter, no matter what color, creed, or beliefs you might have.

That Stinks

I do not have what you might refer to as an iron stomach. Certain things I cannot tolerate. A freshly hocked loogie, for example, or anything remotely having to do with sinus evacuation, is enough to make me want to run far away.

One day, more than twenty years ago now, I had a customer bring in his little boy for an appointment. In the middle of the child's haircut, he turned into a water fountain, opening his mouth and projectile vomiting in a manner resembling a lawn sprinkler. I assure you what came from deep within this boy looked nothing like water. In fact, there was some macaroni, some beef tips, and what may have been a tube of Chap Stick. Seriously though, I got a very good look as I glanced at the pool that had formed in the ashtray of my barbering chair. Even now, it is hard for me to describe without dry heaving.

His father panicked, running out of the shop toward the corner store to purchase a few heave duty cleaning products. Considering that afterward, I felt like the very matter that had pooled in my ashtray, you certainly understand that I could not help Dad clean the rancid mess. I won't allow myself to even begin to describe the stench.

The kid ended up being all right, though. In fact, when Dad got back with the supplies, his boy said, "I feel much better now, Daddy." That made one of us.

The Barbershop Quartet

My girls and I have worked hard together to keep the Progressive Barbershop afloat for all these many years. Each one of us has put in long hours over many years to provide the best service for our loyal customers. Ro, Linda, Sue, and Karen are the reason I am the success that I am today. I think this might be a good opportunity to provide for you a better picture of each of these eccentric young women:

LINDA

Linda is the strange type; one of those Gonzo-type people that Hunter S. Thompson used to refer to as too strange to live, but too rare to die. She garbs herself with clothing most of us baby boomers still have stashed away somewhere in the corners of our attics. Flower power still blooms in her heart, just beneath her tribal patterned sundresses of brown and beige. She is a living relic for new generations of hippie people and cheap love (I say cheap because these days, nothing is *free*).

Consistent with all of this, Linda believes that she was a Native American in a former life, and that she will return again in another life to fulfill her dharmic obligations to the divine creator, whoever *that* may be. In the eyes of her and her late husband, Mike, Kris Kristofferson is the divine creator. They have been to so many of his concerts that he actually knows them by name!

As you may have already guessed, Linda is a raging animal lover. She did not speak to me for a week after I sucked up some ants into the shop vacuum cleaner. She even scolded my youngest son one time for pulling the leaves off of an artificial plant at the shop. Yeah, it's like that.

Linda has a strong passion for fine wine and food. She has never been on time for anything in her life, ever. Her regular customers actually come in for their appointments fifteen minutes late in anticipation of having to wait. And to be honest, they do not ever seem to mind. This is a testament to her incredibly wonderful and at times infectious personality. Everybody should be so lucky as to have an employee as caring and as special as Linda.

So what if she is the clumsiest stoner you have ever met; so what is she gets an infection from a paper cut on her foot and can't walk for a full week; so what if she once got bees up her pant leg while she was out for a walk and took them off in the middle of the road to set them free. What I would have given to be a motorist in Prattsburg that day! So what about all of those things when you consider that she has been there for me for basically my entire life, helping me by personally demonstrating all the wrong decisions a person could possibly make (intentionally, I am sure) so that I could make better ones for myself. I love you, Linda.

RO

Fifteen years ago, I met Ro at a Christmas party a mutual friend was having. We got to talking about the barber shop, and by the end of that first conversation, I had convinced her that apprenticing under me at the shop would be a great idea. It was one of the best professional and personal decisions I have ever made. Today, she is an exceptional barber. She was, after all, taught by the very best (*toot, toot*). It is also interesting to me that things have worked out so well with Ro, being as how she is as conservative and strait as Linda is liberal and crooked (in the very best way, of course).

Ro sings in a barbershop quartet, is active in her church, and loves to gamble; the very epitome of conservative. She spends time between haircuts donning her husband's socks, singing tunes with no melody, and sweeping hair at one hundred miles an hour on an engine that runs off of coffee.

Professionally, her approach to customers is…well…unique. Ro is a talker. If you are blessed enough to have such a fine barber cut your hair, it is inevitable that she will extract all of your most personal information from you, down to where you buy your underwear, if, indeed, you are wearing underwear at all.

You can imagine how a typical day at the shop might look with Ro and Linda working in adjacent chairs. There's Ro, spending the better part of fifteen minutes with her electric lint brush, going over her sweaters again and again and again. And there is Linda, finally snapping at her, saying in a less than passive voice, "Shut those goddamn things off before I go out of my f*in' mind!" Oh, what a pair.

Ro is always on time, and very organized. She even has a to-do list and has been known to carry a mini tape recorder to keep her thought organized. I am not sure if this is a reflection of her organization, but she had her three children all in the same month, and all in the same week of that month. Now that's planning!

But as different as they may seem on the surface, Ro and Linda are actually quite similar in a lot of strange ways. Like Linda, Ro has a sharp tongue when it comes to other peoples' ill behaved children. She is right up front with how she expects them to behave in the chair, and it is her brashness that shuts them right up, and they end up acting like little angels. Like Linda, Ro never complains, even though she has a second job working many hours at Kodak. Ro also has an intimate knowledge of food and fine wines.

Basically, Ro is a perfect complement to Linda, and a perfect fit at the shop. I am lucky to have met her all those years ago, and I am glad to call her my friend and colleague.

SUE

Sue and I knew each other in high school many, many years ago. Imagine how surprised I was when I ran into her on a street corner, only to find out that we were neighbors in the city. She lived next door to Gary and me on Harper Street. To make a long story short, I convinced Sue to apprentice under me at the barber shop much like I would do with Ro years later. This ended up being one of those great decisions I sometimes made. Not only did our friendship flourish, but Sue worked with me for more than twenty wonderful years.

Sue is a master of all trades. Whatever she tries, she succeeds in. She taught Arts and Crafts at the college level; she created her own line of clothing; and she once even reupholstered my sofa.

She is a talented seamstress, and her artistic nature is evident throughout all aspects of her life. Some of Sue's artistic ideas go beyond the depth of human understanding. Whether it be designing jewelry or decorating her home, Sue is an eccentric. For her to wear a necklace adorned with chicken bones and her own baby teeth would not be beyond the realm of possibilities. She always dresses in layers upon layers of elegant clothing and wears rings on every finger. She cuts and perms her own hair, makes her own pet treats, fixes her own car and wears Petrulli oil for perfume. Her sense of humor can be very dry, but she really is a stitch. She has no patience for stupidity and will not tolerate inappropriate behaviors from anyone, kids or adults, men or women. Her garden is a menagerie of herbs and majestic flowers. Whatever she touches, grows. The success of my shop cacti is largely due to Sues loving care.

She has strong opinions on everything from politics to windmills and always stands strong for her convictions. I really admire her for that. Aside from Sue being my son's Godmother, she is one of the most talented and finest people that I have known and had the pleasure to work with for so many years.

KAREN

Karen came to the shop fresh out of barbering school. Although Sue, Ro, and Linda are like family, Karen actually is my sister-in-law. Not surprisingly, her quick wit and raunchy humor made her a great addition to the shop.

Karen is the youngest of the girls at the shop, and by far the thinnest. Truth be told, the rest of us (excluding Sue) look like manatees next to Karen. Her slight build is in no way reflective of her monster work ethic or her hardened personality, however. Karen is a great worker. If ever there is down time between customers, Karen always finds helpful ways to pass the time. After a cigarette and a quick cell phone conversation, she might re-sweep the floors, or vacuum the carpets, or cleanse the bathroom, or wash and fold the towels.

I think her work ethic is the result of all the badass jobs she has worked in the past. She has been in the landscaping business; she has worked with heavy machinery beneath a sweltering August sun in New York. Karen is a woman first, however. Remember she is about 26 pounds soaking wet, with blonde hair and pretty brown eyes. She actually owns pink steel-toed work boots, a pink hard-hat, and pink tools. She is an interesting mesh of Gwen Stefani and Randy Quaid.

Although Karen may appear slight, beware the rage! As is the case with most undersized women, do not piss her off! Her tiny elbows are like daggers; her fists like rock hammers. But, I'll be damned if those hammers don't give the best facials and shaves in the city. In the business today, being able to give a good straight razor shave and facial is very rare. Karen has been a real asset to the shop. Her drive and determination are without comparison.

A Little Slice of Lice

One of the most difficult tasks to tackle in my profession is knowing how to back away from a head full of lice eggs without embarrassing the client or alarming the rest of the customers in the shop. Luckily, this does not happen that often; but, it *does* happen.

One time, I stumbled across what looked to be a settlement of little animals in this customer's hair. The creatures were hoarded around enough unhatched lice eggs to build the world's biggest omelet. Gross! Luckily, there were no other customers in the shop at the time. I politely told the man that I would not be able to do his haircut until he consulted an exterminator. I recommended *Mr. Quell*.

To this day, I cannot understand how this man, and others like him, did not realize that there is a tiny city of parasites nesting within their hair. I would imagine the itching would be unbearable. I spent the next hour sterilizing my equipment and washing my hands. The guy must have been pretty embarrassed because I never did see him again.

Is there a Dentist in the House?

I think Chuck, our family dentist, and I had been discussing the high suicide rate in the dental profession when the accident occurred. We both rushed from the shop into the street outside to tend to the victims involved.

When we got close, we saw that one of the women was upside down in the front seat of her car. Her head was in the leg area and her feet were dangling confusedly over the head rest of the passenger seat. I have no idea how she could have ended up in this position, but that is the way we found her.

When we saw her face, we noticed she was bleeding profusely from somewhere. Chuck reacted immediately, and I played the role of Johnny-on-the-spot, getting towels and gloves and anything else Chuck said he could use to tend to the woman.

He was great. He applied pressure to the wound, held her head still, and reassured her that help was on the way, and that she was going to be fine. Everything Chuck had told the woman ended up being true, although we later found out that she did require a modest amount of stitches to close the gap that had opened her upper lip. Good old Chuck.

He can drill my teeth anytime; just so long as he gives me enough Novocain to keep me drooling for a weekend.

Judge Not, Lest Ye' be judged

I won't lie to you and act like I don't ever use my friends to get me out of different jams, because I do. I have dropped names of judges, lawyers, policemen, doctors, elected officials, plumbers, and housewives to get out of a variety of traffic tickets over the years. After an experience I had years ago, however, I am much more careful about who I share my stories with.

Many years ago, when I was still in the original shop, I had gotten pulled over for speeding on my way into work. I tried my best to get out of it, explaining that I had been trying to pass a tractor trailer that had been driving erratically in front of me. I explained that it looked like there was a gremlin behind the wheel and surely, someone had been feeding it well after midnight. The cop was not amused.

Neither was the judge. When I got to court, he was not trying to hear my pleading. In fact, he was not trying to hear any of us. He was writing fines like Anna Nicole's doctor writes prescriptions. We all paid dearly that day.

The next week a new customer came into the shop and in the course of our conversation, I began telling him about my ordeal with this arrogant, pompous judge, and how he loved sticking it to everyone in the court room. As I was cashing the guy out he handed me his business card. I did a double take. Ironically his last name was the same as the judge's. Barely able to mumble the words, I managed to say "Are you by any chance related?" Of course, he replied, "I'm his first born". I wanted to disappear. If only I could be the fly on the wall instead of the barber with the foot in her mouth.

Words were not going to make this better, so I said nothing. HEY, AWK--WARD! He paid and left. Years later he showed up at my shop again, not realizing that I had moved to a new location. I never forget a face. Evidently, he doesn't either. He requested one of the other girls to cut his hair and I never saw him again. Whatever happened to forgive and forget? I was only trying to pass a tractor trailer!!

I'll stop, I swear

There are a few uncanny similarities between my barbershop and my mechanic's garage; namely, the f*in' language. I'll be first to tell you that I curse like a naval Admiral. In fact, as I write this book, I continue going back time after time to clean up some of the statements I have made. This is, after all, meant to be a family book. The shop on the other hand, with some exceptions, is a man's place. It has to be in order to appeal to the clientele. That said, rarely does my filthy language offend.

I am Catholic, however, and sometimes I inadvertently use the Lord's name in vain. Sometimes, I even feel guilty. You gotta' love that about religion, right? Anyway, in 2000, I decided that giving up swearing was going to be my New Year's resolution. Some of the guys at the shop laughed at me for the mere suggestion that this was possible. I'd show them.

One customer actually organized a parley based on how long it would be before I broke my resolution. This only strengthened my resolve to succeed. I even took a few bets against free haircuts that I could succeed.

The first week was a cakewalk; no problem at all. It was like God was helping me with my resolution by removing all life's little hurdles. My kids did not get arrested that week, there were no traffic tickets, no physical injuries, and all in all, things went smooth.

The second week was a bit harder, however. There were a few close calls, but I stayed strong, biting my tongue when the urge to spew filth came over me. There were a few difficult customers, some irritating telemarketers, and even a lost article of clothing. I had made it, though. And like a quitting smoker, I figured that the second week was surely the hardest, and from now on, it would have to be smooth sailing. This was not the case.

My resolve began to weaken considerably at the beginning of week three. My nerves were jumpy, and I even began to talk less to the customers just so that the likelihood of me cussing would be less. Things were not looking good. As week three came to an end, something terrible happened - the dreaded pointer-knuckle snip. I guess my nerves got the best of me as my razor sharp shears cut through the fatty part of my left index finger like a hot knife through butter. Holy sh*t did it hurt! And I let everybody hear about it with a plethora of four letter words.

You would have thought someone had hit the *Powerball* jackpot. My customers began celebrating like they had been elected prom queens; and for good reason. I had to give about five dozen freebees to clients who had bet against me. I'm proud to tell you not *everybody* bet against me. I do have a couple of Mormons who are forbidden to bet due to their religion; but, I like to think they actually believed in me (yeah, right).

I'll always remember how well I did for almost three full weeks that January. And when I am ready, I will give it another try, but this time I will succeed, and they will all be paying me back what they took before. I swear it! Oops.

Without a Net

Back when I first opened my own shop, I decided to offer discount haircuts with the hopes of expanding my clientele. I lowered the price of progressive haircuts from 4.50 to 3.75. God, things were so different back then. Today I struggle to stay afloat charging 15.00 for a haircut. Anyway, within a week I started receiving nasty and threatening phone calls from anonymous callers warning me to stop undercutting other barber shops in and around the city.

It did not take long for me to figure out who was behind the threats. I had gone out on a limb and went against union against the established union rules. Being young, naïve, and inexperienced at the time, I complied mostly out of fear. At the time, I couldn't afford to have my windows broken! And cutting hair with two broken legs is something that has never really appealed to me. Years went by, and as I grew older and wiser, I vowed never to allow myself to be strong-armed by anyone again, ever.

It's 2004, I'm 54 years old and the archaic practices of the old barbers union have died with the stuffy old-timers that founded it so many years ago. Why, then, am I feeling a sense of déjà vu?

In early 2004, I received a letter from the city, informing me that city council had passed an addition to an existing piece of legislation concerning small businesses within the city. This legislation was called the *Certificate of Use,* or C of U. They now required that ***all*** retail businesses with 20,000 square feet or less to get a *Certificate of Use*. If any business did not get one, they would inevitably face strict disciplinary measures, including having their businesses closed down. As I soon found out, the city council's goal was to systematically rid the city of bad businesses; that is, businesses that had been participating in illegal activities (i.e. drug dealing, gambling, prostitution). The existing laws, apparently, were not working fast enough, nor were they effective enough. The city empowered an existing faction of local government to enforce the new legislation. It was called the NET, or *Neighborhood Empowerment Teams*. The whole thing sounds almost reasonable, doesn't it? Please, allow me to continue…

The NET had been established a few years earlier to allow city residents to carry out standard city business and to address a variety of neighborhood issues in what amounted to miniature city halls located within their own neighborhoods. "Standard business" included things like getting a hunting license, or issuing a formal complaint about your neighbor's unkempt lawn. There were six NET offices located throughout the city. Still sounds like a reasonable and potentially productive operation, yes?

This legislation had some serious problems, and was to become one of the most contentious issues I've run into in all my years as a small business owner. At one point, I felt so mistreated by the city regarding the Certificate of Use, that I actually considered moving the shop up the street 2 blocks, out of city limits where the C of U was not required.

Let me start by saying that in its original drafted form, the C of U required that all business owners be "of good moral character." Herein lays one of the fundamental errors in the whole C of U concept. Who, after all, is qualified to determine what it means to be of good moral character? I remind you that same-sex marriage was not recognized in the state of New York at the time. Were the same folks who petitioned against the recognition of same-sex marriages going to be those who were deemed qualified to make moral judgments? You can see how an openly gay business owner might have reservations about this possibility. Not surprisingly, this verbiage, and similar nonsensical statements, had been amended before I was even aware of the new legislation.

One thing the city did not change when finalizing this legislation was the fact that the city council gave the NET the authority to do whatever *they* felt was necessary to meet their ultimate goal - to get rid of bad businesses. This small tributary of local government had been given a blank check, so to speak; a check they were not shy about cashing. What, I ask, has history taught us about giving an individual unlimited power? I need not remind you of men like Hitler, Stalin, Mussolini, and Cat Stephens.

Along with the required $100 charge, the NET also demanded that all small business owners have their pictures submitted to the city to be kept on record. This picture was also to be displayed with our C of U in our store windows. Imagine a local jeweler's picture on the outside of their shop, certainly helpful for potential thieves to identify who might be carrying the day's profits to the bank at the end of the day. The NET also required social security numbers be available so they could do background checks on business proprietors. For reasons still unclear to me, the NET official also required that I submit a copy of my home phone bill to their officers. Are you starting to understand my growing concern?

Other points to this legislation were even worse. There were several situations stated that could result in the termination of my business. They could shut me down if any of my employees had a parking ticket, or if my landlords didn't pay their taxes. They also placed restrictions on who I was allowed to employ. According to the legislation, employers were not allowed to hire convicted felons. Understand that I am not in the practice of hiring convicted felons, but I believe that decision should not be made for me by others.

As I have suggested before, I am not above using my connections in the city for my own agendas. My contacts in the city newspapers and local television news proved very handy. I managed to schedule a variety of interviews in hopes that I could enlighten the city about the injustices that were befalling their local businesses.

The owner of the pet shop down the street called me to talk about the C of U. She was pissed off, too; and wanted to do something about it. My interviews went very well, and after they were aired on the local news, I started getting calls from many small business owners throughout the city. Many of us decided to meet to discuss what we could do to contest the new laws we felt were unfair.

Over the next several months we met about once a week. Several of the other business owners were also interviewed by the news media and it became quite a news item in Rochester. We all decided to fight together as a group and try to stop this crazy legislation. We created petitions in our respective stores; we had fund raisers to help pay for any legal fees that might have transpired; and many of us blatantly refused to comply with the NET's demands. We all kept our customers well informed, and several times, we (our customers included) even protested on the steps of city hall.

Many of us were being ticketed daily for violating NET policies. At one point I was up to $2800 in fines! The NET enforcers were literally sticking tickets in my door when I wasn't even there to receive them. I would lock my barbershop door and only open it when familiar customers arrived, hoping of keeping the NET bullies out of my shop.

On one occasion, one of these idiots entered my shop under false pretenses. When I identified him as a NET agent, I asked him to leave. The police were called, and when they arrived, the asshole claimed that I assaulted him. He wanted the cops to arrest me! At this point I had Karen snap his picture for evidence. When we had the film developed, it revealed a maniacal bully with his finger pointed at me, and spit flying out of his mouth. I enlarged his picture and put it in my front window at the shop along with a background check I did on him. I also hung all my tickets up next to his photo. I wanted to let the NET know exactly how it felt to be treated like a common criminal. Hell hath no fury, right?

Other businesses followed suit and proceeded to call news people down to my shop to check out my latest window dressings. Good publicity. The local media jumped on it like flies on honey. We became regulars at city council meetings and collectively spoke out against the legislation and the NET. Our coalition actually met with city council members on several different occasions. We even met with the potential new Mayor. As time went on, more and more businesses and people were realizing just how bad the legislation really was and were beginning to ban together with our group. We started our own e-mail address: *Sayno2cofu.com*.

People were responding daily with their opinions, both good and bad. Leave it to the Baby Boomers to bring the 60's back to life-actively protesting the injustices being dealt by local government.

As I have eluded, during this time the mayoral race was heating up in the city. It really became an issue all candidates had to address. The Center for Government Research was requested by city council to evaluate the entire NET program. They had meetings throughout the city with average citizens to find out how they received the NET. Needless to say, we attended these meeting also.

Showing our dissatisfaction!

Just after the election, the report by the C.G.R. came out. Although their prime objective was to evaluate the NET, they had some very interesting things to say about the C. of U. and how badly the NET enforcers were treating people. Soon after the report came out, the new mayor put a hold on the C of U and relinquished power from the NET, and all fines were suspended. Months went by and we all hoped that the issue was dead. After all, the whole situation painted Rochester to be a less-than-desirable place to start a small business.

Although some of the new council members were against it, city council re-issued a modified version of the C of U. They even tried to cloak this new certificate in a new name, calling it a "Business Permit." They did eliminate some of the most ridiculous provisions, but it was still a terrible idea.

But, after haggling about it for several more weeks, city council passed it. Now the fee was $25.00 instead of $100. The city even began writing refunds for those businesses that had paid the original $100. Rest assured; I was not one of them.

Is that not incredible? They modified enough of the law so that the group as a whole decided to go along. Truth be told, I think most of the team folded out of sheer exhaustion. Anyway, don't think you can't make a difference; and do not think that you are powerless. All you need is conviction, determination, and hippies, and you can change the world…well…the city anyway. We tried and consider ourselves victors. We single-handedly changed a law, reshaped local government, and made the city a better place for businesses, which in turn, makes the city a better place for our customers. ***Flower power!***

Whair does it hurt?

In most professions, perfection comes at a price. Baseball players risk taking fastballs to the face and body; policemen frequently deal with dangerous people toting guns, knives, and a variety of other weapons; seamstresses—well, you get the point. The barbering trade has its hardships, as well. You might not know this, but something as miniscule as a whisker can cause unfathomable pain when lodged in the fleshy skin between the little piggy that went to the market, and the little piggy that came home. Loose hairs are like hollow needles that seem to prefer to take refuge in the most sensitive and tender spots on the body.

My husband and I were in this furniture store browsing around one evening. I had been complaining incessantly about this pain that shot up my heel every time I took a step. It felt like a piece of glass was inside my sock, slowly burrowing itself deeper and deeper within the nerve endings of my foot as I continued walking through the store.

I consider myself to have a pretty healthy pain threshold, but the point came where I actually had to sit down. I undressed my foot, hoping to reveal the culprit; and not surprisingly, there it was! There, sticking out of my heel like an extension chord, was a solitary brown hair. Now, this came as no surprise to me, for this kind of thing happened all the time. Usually, I just have Gary tweeze the little buggers out. This hair was unique, however. I could tell by the look on my husband's face when he extracted it. He had a look of nausea mixed with contempt. I asked him what the matter was.

Apparently, this hair was different. It was embedded a good inch into the meaty part of my heel. Gary looked like a circus clown pulling 50 meters of fabric from his breast pocket. He yanked on it again and again. God, did it feel good when it was finally out.

A few years ago, Linda actually had a tiny piece of hair sticking in her sclera – or, the white part of the eye. I was nervous when she asked me to pull the little guy out. I'm old, after all; shaky; and my eyes are bad. Besides, there was always the possibility that her brains could have leaked out the hole after the hair was removed, right?

The boob is the worse place to be pierced by a hair, though. Of course, it is also the place where hairs most commonly get stuck. Every time you move your bra irritates it even more and imbeds it deeper and deeper, like a Novocain needle without the payoff. You need to scream, but you don't want to alert the customer about the malady. So, in agony, you quickly finish the haircut and hope the guy will leave pretty fast so that you can disappear into the bathroom and disrobe, much like Superman, to remove the thorn.

God forbid a hair puncture gets infected. Linda's finger got infected so badly one time as the result of a hair barb, she had to go to the doctor and get the puss squeezed out of what had become a swollen red balloon-knuckle. Delicious! Bottom line, there are times when I would much prefer a high-and-tight 99 mph fastball to a course chin hair in my bra.

Knuckle Down

My scissors are sharpened three times a year. A man comes to the barber shop every four months with a van fully equipped with shear-sharpening tools. In a matter of no more than twenty minutes, he has them sharpened and ready for use. It's quite convenient.

In addition to unwanted hairs being lodged in your body, the combination of knuckle skin and newly sharpened scissors can also pose a real risk in my profession. You're always a little paranoid when first using freshly sharpened scissors, knowing that one slip could completely remove the flesh on either of your most important fingers. It has happened to all barbers at one time or another, regardless of how good they are. It is inevitable. You hold the hair with one hand and use the other hand to snip the hair. If you're not careful - trouble!

Believe me when I tell you that the knuckles bleed like hell. And, they take forever to heal because you are constantly bending your fingers. It's like when you burn the inside of your lip, but it won't heal because you can't stop tonguing it. And, even though you put a Band Aid on it, by the end of the day you still manage to get hair stuck in the wound. It's really disgusting, considering how filthy hair generally is. By my late twenties, my hands looked like they belonged to *Leatherface* from *The Texas Chainsaw Massacre*.

Playing the Odds

Through the years I've come across some pretty strange people at the barber shop. This one man used to come in for a haircut, stipulating that I didn't touch his scalp with the comb or a brush. I would have to lift his hair with only my fingers and then cut it. He also insisted on wearing eye blinders (or patches) during the process. He must have heard about Linda's sclera fiasco. It would take me forever to finish his hair. He looked totally ridiculous! I often wondered if he was asleep under those eye patches. Maybe he was just imagining that I was Angelina Jolie, or Joan Rivers, or Al Roker.

I had another client that was equally strange. His hair always had a strange film on it. I figured it was some kind of hair product that he applied and that I was not familiar with. It turns out it was his own unique hair rinse… it was his own urine! I almost puked. He said it was supposed to be healthy for the hair; it added sheen. He must have been out of his mind. One thing is for sure… he certainly *pissed* me off! I always like to have a heads–up if I'm going to be wrist deep in excrement. I do not think I hid my displeasure very well, because he stopped coming to the shop. I wonder if his new barber knows the reason for his hair's superior luster.

I recall this one guy named Roy who frequently came to the shop. He was extremely wealthy and a very generous tipper. He always wore a big cowboy hat, complete with cowboy belt and boots. The bottoms of his boots had taps on them so we could hear him coming a mile away. As is often the case with the wealthy, he never had a problem flaunting his money. And in this case, the girls and I did no t mind even a little bit. It was standard for him to leave a $40 tip on a $15 haircut. We would all drool when we'd see him coming, fighting each other to decide on who was going to service him (not like *that*, perverts). Sometimes, we would flip a coin to see who would be the lucky one to cut his hair; or, we would race to see how fast we could finish the client in our chair so that we could get to Roy as soon as he walked through the door. I usually won these little competitions, often sacrificing spectacular haircuts, for just plain great ones. When it comes to money, after all, I am Speedy Gonzales.

It was not just that Roy had money; or even that he tipped so big. Most other wealthy clients have to wait just like anyone else. Roy is a very special person, however. One of my cousins is part of a local search and rescue team. Their organization assists the police in looking for fugitives, victims, missing persons, and lost children. Roy once bought my cousin a very expensive Blood Hound to aide her team. It is actions like this that make the girls and me want to help Roy. Well…that and the money, of course!

The Peoples' Court

Have you ever wondered what it would be like to be on one of those televised court shows? I came real close to being on one of them, once. It all started when I contracted a repairman to fix one of my barbering chairs.

He did a fine job. He was quick, and made the experience as convenient for me as could be. His workmanship was great, as well. My positive experience with this man led me to contract him to fix another one of my chairs. Again, he came to get the chair; this time, however, I did not hear from him for several weeks. When I finally did get in touch with him, he assured me that the chair would be done soon, and he would be returning it promptly afterward. He did.

He returned the chair on a Saturday; coincidentally a day that I do not typically work. Needless to say, I was not there to inspect the chair upon its return. I did not see the chair, as a matter of fact, until I opened the shop the following Monday morning. I thought it was strange that the chair was still sitting on a dolly. I inspected the chair more closely, finding that not only was it no repaired, but there were several pieces missing, as well. The fact is the chair was in worse shape that when I sent it out; it was unusable!

I called him numerous times. The man (Ben, we'll call him) promised me over and over that he would make good on our agreement with the chair. I was still willing to give him the benefit of the doubt, even though I already knew a favorable outcome was unlikely. After a few weeks, Ben refused to take my calls and made no further efforts to resolve the matter.

You may be thinking, "Hey, they're only chairs, for God's sake."

You have to understand that these chairs were over 60 years old. They are very rare, and very expensive. Not only do they represent the history of the Progressive Barbershop, but they are also relics that represent the time that I have personally been affiliated with it. My attachment to the chairs is just as much sentimental as it is financial.

Anyway, I decided to wait one more week. When nothing was resolved I decided to take it to small claims court. As the court documents were going through, I received a certified letter in the mail from a producer of a syndicated Court TV show. They thought my case sounded interesting, and wanted me to present it in front of a camera crew in a television courthouse in New York City. The hotel and accompanying accommodations would have been paid for had I decided to do it. Unfortunately, if I had done it, the network would have covered a large portion of Ben's fines. That is the way those court shows work, you know. Pay attention next time one of them is on. There is usually a very brief disclaimer explaining how the majority of administered fines are covered by the producers and the network, and the defendants get off easy simply for showing up. I decided not to let Ben off that easy, and declined the tantalizing invite. Cue small claims court.

I figured since I was having no luck resolving the issue myself, maybe a judge could help. Not surprisingly, Ben did not show up in court, and I automatically won the case. My lawyer put a freeze on his bank accounts, and took the money out, not needing to inform or warn him. Although I had been compensated financially, I hardly felt good about the outcome. Do me a favor, *don't touch the chair*!

O-Minus Twelve Hours

I may have said this before, but for those of you who have just opened this book to this page, I will let you know that I am a huge pet lover. A few years ago I had a client who was looking for a good home for his one year old wiener dog. We had recently lost our dog Daisy to cancer, and were silently longing for another pup. Of course, I expressed my interest in adopting his dog. Before he would even consider this, he insisted on having an interview with me to determine if I would be the best parent to his pet. Jack was a traveling salesman, and felt that he was not able to spend enough time caring for the dog. He wanted to find a home for the dog where it would get the attention he thought it needed. I totally understood and agreed to talk to him further on the subject.

I explained to him that my husband and I loved animals and have always had and loved our dogs. I told him that our kids had been raised around animals and, between us all, that there would always be people around to keep the dog company, and give it the attention he thought it needed. I told him that we had a large, fenced-in backyard where the dog could run free instead of being in a crate for hours every day. The guy felt very comfortable with me and decided we would be good responsible owners of his dog. I was thrilled!

We named him Oscar. The name was quite fitting for a wiener dog. He took to his new home immediately. He even slept in our bed the first night in his new house. Dangerous, considering my husband outweighed him by 230 pounds. But, things were fine, and I went to work the next day feeling excited about our new family member. Oh, how things were about to change.

Around 4:00 that afternoon I got a phone call from my son Gabriel begging me to come home. I could hear my other son, Nathaniel, sobbing uncontrollably in the background. Apparently, Oscar had run out of the house and into the street and got hit by a school bus. A school bus! Nathaniel had chased him outside, and was within two feet from reaching him when the bus hit Oscar. Nathaniel was understandably devastated, feeling responsible for the accident. Not to mention, he had just witnessed his 6 pound puppy get shattered by a large capacity vehicle.

I immediately left a half-finished haircut and sped home.

After attempting to console my teenage son (with little success, by the way), I immediately began thinking about how I was going to break the news to the nice gentleman from whom I had gotten the dog. I knew he would be calling to check up on the puppy soon enough.

I initially thought about writing him a letter and explaining what had happened. I would make it sound very heartfelt and hope he would understand. I was so upset by this time that the girls from the barber shop had to come to my house to calm me down. How was I to tell this man that his beautiful dog lasted a measly twelve hours in our Death House!

After reconsidering the whole thing, I came to the conclusion that the best thing to do was to lie through my teeth. I'm pathetic and the world's biggest chicken and I'll just have to live with that. This could very possibly be my condemnation to hell. But, I was willing to take that chance. The next day I went to work with my evil plan in place, and nervously waited for his phone call. Sure as hell, within an hour the phone rang. The first question out of his mouth was, "How's my little buddy doing?" I cautiously replied, "Fine." The guy was really happy and relieved.

Within about a second I suddenly got hysterical and was crying my eyes out into the phone. I found myself blurting the whole tragic story to him. For too long, there was silence on the other end of the line. In a less than convincing way, he finally said that he understood; and that obviously, it had been an accident. I decided to still send the letter to him the next day hoping to rid myself of any remaining feelings of guilt. I never heard from, or saw the guy again after that. But I must say, even to this day every time I have a pain in my body I have visions of this man sticking needles in a voodoo doll he calls *Pattie*!

You Get What You Pay For

Owning a barbershop on one of the city's most popular avenues has had its advantages. One of those advantages is independent vendors. These salespeople come into the shop from time to time, selling merchandise of all kinds, from alarm clocks to suitcases. I am a firm believer that local businesses should utilize each other's services, so I frequently buy from these traveling salespeople. I remember one winter I bought half a dozen hardcover cookbooks that I wrapped and gave as holiday gifts. I even included cookies with the books-cookies that I made using a recipe from the book! A great idea if I may say so, myself; and thrifty, for the books only cost me five dollars apiece.

As you might assume, not all merchandise purchased from street vendors are of such outstanding quality. A young man once came into the shop selling dress socks by the dozen for a measly three dollars. I figured, "What the hell?" I bought three dozen pairs. So what if they were not of the best quality, three dollars a dozen was still a steal. And I was right; but, it was *him* stealing from *me*!

I took a bucketful of these hideous socks home to my husband, and as he tried them on, pair by pair, he ripped every heel out of every sock he put on his feet. Every pair! They must have used corn silk for the threading. What a rip off (no pun intended)!

That incident has not dissuaded me from continuing to give the local venders my business. I understand that it must be a tough way to make a living, especially considering that the venders, themselves, only get a portion of the money they earn every day. Even though the venders do make a commission, most of the money venders make goes to the corporate office. I respect these people, however. They are not at home, living off the system; but instead they are out working their butts off, trying to make ends meet. So I urge you, support your local salesmen, but be prepared, for you most often get what you pay for.

Frankly, My Deer…

With the gas crisis in full swing, I often fanaticize about how great it would be if scientists could figure out a way to convert hair trimmings into energy. Think about that; an organic source of energy that will surely never be exhausted. You could shave in the morning, and your whiskers could provide you with enough fuel to get to work! Or maybe a company could use it to stuff pillows, or insulate a house. Over the years, I have thought of about a million different practical uses for discarded human hair.

You can imagine my curiosity when a man came into the shop requesting that I bag all my discarded hair for him to pick up at the end of the week. I remember thinking this man either had figured out a concrete way to convert hair into something wonderful; or, he was some kind of sick pervert who would spread the hair all over his chest after the sun went down as part of some twisted sex ritual. I could not be responsible for feeding the man's sickness, so I asked him how he was going to use the hair. His response was something that I had never even considered.

Apparently, varmints had taken his vegetable garden hostage, and he was going to put human hair around the perimeter of his plants because the scent, he believed, would deter the animals. He explained that it was so effective; it would scare away everything from raccoons, to fuzzy bunnies, to deer. Genius! It must have worked, because the man never came in again.

That night I filled up my own garbage bag, praying that come the holidays, sprinkling some of my customer's hair at the end of our driveway might deter the in-laws from coming to the house. Hey, I'll try anything!

One of my favorite things to do in my spare time is to make "hair hounds". You wait until you have a decent amount of hair on the floor, and then you mold a dog! Depending on how much hair you have depends on the size of your dog. Sometimes you have to settle for a puppy. You can put collars on them made out of bread twists or use gum balls for their eyes. They look like the real thing. One day, my friend Sue, took some pictures of our "hair hounds", and got the bright idea to send them in to the David Letterman show. We were hoping, because of his known fondness of dogs, that he would invite us to be on his show. Maybe even cut his hair and, wallah! Twice we sent the photos, but no luck. What a bummer.

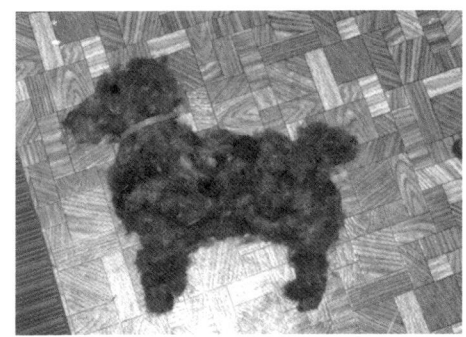

I also have a wall in the shop that has a dozen or so of discarded "tails". When a guy gets tired of his long hair, and wants to cut it off, I comply and display it with the others on the wall. Each tail is unique. There's very long ones; short ones, curly ones, frizzy ones and full and thin ones. There's tails of many different colors and some are dirty and some are clean. Every tail has a tale. If you're bored of your long hair, please, let us keep it on our wall as a reminder of your hairier days.

The "Tails"

It's the Most Wonderful Time of the Year

I'm probably not the only one whose favorite time of the year is Christmas. But I am fortunate in that every year, without fail, I get to see so much good from such a large cross-section of Rochester city residents. The majority of my clients bring gifts, not just for the girls and me, but for anyone who may come into the shop. Some of the more popular gifts are booze, candy, homemade cookies, and gift certificates. Jan, the mail lady, can even more easily coaxed into singing a carol or two while customers top off their coffees with *Bailey's Irish Cream.* God, how I love my extended family. One weekend this last holiday season, we went through about five bottles of *Bailey's* and about half as many pots of coffee. I still can't figure it out; but it is happenings like this that make me want to celebrate the birth of the Lord every day of the year.

One other instance stands out in my mind; and incident that demonstrates perfectly the joy of the season. From time to time, it snows in Rochester, New York. If you are not from the region, you might not fully understand my sarcasm. It freakin' snows like crazy in Rochester. It's cold; it's wet; it's unavoidable. Usually, the snow makes people miserable. One year as Christmas approached, a moderate flurry had blanketed the sidewalk outside the shop. A perfect stranger came in as the sun began to fade, asking if he could shovel the walkway for me. Delighted by the gesture, I said yes. Looking out as the man was working, I noticed that he was not wearing gloves and did not have a hat. Out of his own volition, the man was doing me a favor, shoveling my sidewalk in the blistering cold.

The kicker is, he returned a few days later to help me out again. Little did he know that Santa had visited the shop in the meantime, leaving a gift addressed to the helpful stranger. Santa had apparently seen the man's good deed and left for him a gift of woolen gloves and a winter hat. I was glad to contribute something to the spirit of the holiday. Merry Christmas, stranger.

Bartender, How About Another!

We don't mix martinis, and we don't pour body shots, but in many ways barbers are a lot like bartenders. We both inevitably make ourselves available to listen to peoples' problems, and too often, our opinions are welcome. At times, I feel like I should be getting paid a psychiatrist's salary for my infinite wisdom. My track record with giving advice might help to explain why I am a barber and not a licensed mental health professional.

A gentleman came into the shop one time, obviously down about something. It did not take mush prodding before the man began blurting out his situation. He had married a woman whom he loved very much. The problem: she was lousy as hell in bed. She was cold as a cucumber, and about as engaging as a picture frame. Why he married her was beyond me. If this was something that was so important to him, why did he not test the water before jumping into the pond? Because there were no waves, I imagine.

Anyway, for the next few visits, he put the same old sob story on me. It had not gotten any better and it was severely bothering him. Half-kiddingly, I suggested the man have an affair, suggesting that maybe it was just he who was lousy. The man was appalled at my suggestion, but his dismay quickly turned into something else: consideration, maybe?

The next time the guy came in he looked like a new man. He was smiling as if he had just come from the gag factory. As it turned out, he had taken my advice to heart. He had had an affair with a woman in his office. Oh God, what had I done! In his excited state, he did not seem to remember that you cannot burn a candle at both ends. It just does not work. Oh well…too late. He now found himself in love with both women, which was unfortunate because when they found out what was going on, they both kicked him to the curb. Ouch! He became suicidal; and where he used to see a professional shrink once a week, and a barber twice a month, he began seeing a shrink thrice a week, and no longer confided in his surrogate bartender. A shock.

Another gentleman, this time elderly, wanted my advice on whether or not he should dye his hair. Ridiculous. The man had been born some time during the Roosevelt administration, after all. Teddy Roosevelt! "Why not," I told him, "If you want to try it, then why not give it a go?" Another bad decision.

The guy comes in a few weeks later with a ridiculous black pompadour on the top of his wrinkly old brow. At least he knew how bad it looked. He was so upset. He had not considered how funny he would look with bleach blonde eyebrows and hair as black as pitch. What a mess. It took four haircuts before the dye came out. Needless to say, the old man no longer asks for my opinions on anything more important than the best route to the Post Office.

I'd almost feel guilty, but then I consider that I make $15 a haircut, and not $200.00 an hour. Again, you get what you pay for. Sorry all.

Watt?

The lighting in the barbershop isn't the best, especially during the winter months when the skies are always overcast. Rochester is not known for its vast amount of sunny days. I make due by putting extra high-wattage lamps in the shop. Aside from creating more light, they also make the shop seem cozier. It is amazing how light translates to happiness. I have one lamp at each of the girl's stations.

I'm cutting hair one day when I smell something burning. The smell got progressively worse over time, but no one could figure out where it was coming from. A few minutes pass, when I notice the melting plastic lamp shade, smoking. It had a hole in it the size of a tennis ball!

Apparently, the wattage of the bulb was too high for the size of the lamp and it caught the shade on fire. I almost burned the damn shop down. The fumes were enough to make you sick. Always looking to save a buck, I kept the lamp and began telling people that it was art deco-style. It looked *so* ridiculous, people would have to believe me. Would you believe that there were some people that actually did? A few even asked where I had bought it. Artsy people make me laugh.

Anyway, I upped my fire insurance in the shop and continued to use 150 watt light bulbs. Let there be light!

Why So Crotchety?

I'm eight years old when it comes to spray bottles. I have had this spraying fetish ever since I was a kid. Especially now, I love watching how people react when I turn the gun on them. Some vow to get even, but in the end, they usually do not. When they do try to defend themselves, we usually end up saturating the whole barber shop and anything (or any one) else in our path.

One of my favorite things to do to my pal Linny is to saturate the back of her pants while she's doing a haircut…unbeknown to her, of course. You have to set the nozzle in such a way that it sprays a soft but steady stream of water. If done properly, Linda won't even catch on until the water has seeped through her apron, her pants, and finally, her undies. It is at this point that all hell usually breaks loose. Lin first reacts to the "cold" spot on her butt, calls me a few choice names, then retaliates. She usually goes right for my face, and I never seem to get my guard up fast enough. More often than not, I take a hard stream of cold water right between my eyes. It's at this point where we turn unprofessional. The poor customers just sit there in amazement, patiently waiting for their haircuts.

Linda is not the only victim of my spray-bottle wrath. On a Tuesday afternoon one of my favorite clients came to get his hair cut. During his cut, we began talking about an upcoming vacation he had been planning. We kept talking even as he stood up, fishing through his packets for money to pay me. He did not notice the dreaded water bottle in my hand at my side. Ever so carefully and quietly did I spray the crotch area of my dear friend's dress pants. After a few minutes he glanced down to see the wet spot and with combined conviction *and* embarrassment he said, "God damn you Pattie!" Why so crotchety, I wondered.

Laura

Running a business in a close knit neighborhood has some nice advantages, one being that eventually you make new friendships with people that you never knew existed. You get to know their kids, their pets and even their relatives. They stop by for coffee, read the paper, watch some TV and enjoy nice conversation. Before you know it lives intertwine, and reaching out to one another, in good times and bad, becomes a vital part of friendships. This brings to mind a very special woman that once lived next door to the barber shop. Her name was Laura. She was a struggling single mom trying her best to raise her young son. The two of them were inseparable. Wherever Laura went, so went her boy. The girls at the shop became very close to both of them and went out of their ways to make them feel welcomed in the neighborhood and in the shop.

On many occasions Laura would seek advice about different things in her life; but mostly pertaining to her son. Being an arbitrator between the two of them became a welcomed occurrence to Laura and we were happy to help out. One day Laura called me at the shop and told me that she found a lump on one of her breasts. She said it was there for eight months and she was scared to see a doctor. I encouraged her to immediately seek medical assistance. A few weeks later it was found to be cancer.

She was scheduled for immediate surgery and began a grueling combination of both chemotherapy and radiation treatment. I remember one day when she called me crying because started to lose her gorgeous long hair. I had her come over to the shop and convinced her to have a buzz-cut, thinking that having no hair at all would be easier to deal with than losing the hair she already had. I told her that until her hair grew back, she might want to go out and get a nice wig. She did exactly that. The horror on her face that I had seen only a few days before completely went away when I saw her wearing that wig.

As time passed, Laura, the girls and I experienced a virtual rollercoaster of highs and lows. She was terribly worried about what would happen to her son if things didn't turn out the way we all prayed that they would. Many times we would just hug each other and pray; poor Laura sobbing into my shoulder. I tried so hard to give her hope, but things progressively became worse.

Within two years Laura lost her battle with cancer and joined God in Heaven, where he surely relieved her of her suffering. Her son Stewart went to live with his father and his family on the other side of the state. I haven't heard from him since, but I think of him a lot. I fear Stewart might be hesitant to see me because of the connection to the memories we shared of his mother's last days. Someday, when our pain has healed, I hope to see him again.

Laura and me

For a long time I felt emptiness in my heart and sadness in my soul having lost Laura. Never seeing her again at my shop was impossible for me to imagine. But, I take some comfort in having known such a kind and wonderful person at all; and, I am glad that we were friends. I look forward to renewing our friendship when we meet again in Heaven.

Cop to This

Home to half a dozen colleges, Rochester has a culturally diverse city, albeit modest in population. It's no New York City, L.A, or Chicago, after all. It does have its similarities to these colossal cities, however. In addition to the honest, hardworking middle-class majority, there are also scum bags, career criminals, ex-cons, and lawyers. You might not know this, but small-city barbershops are where citizens from both sides of the law come to meet. Unintentionally, I am sure.

A detective friend of mine was sitting in the chair one Friday afternoon. Next to me, Linda was giving a haircut to a newer client that I was not familiar with. Detective Bob and I were chewing the fat about this and that, when I noticed Linda's customer squirming around in her chair. I was not really concerned because - believe me - you'd squirm too if you were to entrust your ear lobes to Linda's shaky hands and running mouth. *Maybe the guy is in a hurry*, I remember thinking. *And only this moment has he realized that he might possibly have to sit and listen to Linda's goofy stories deep into the night.* The poor bastard.

She did finally finish. Her customer quietly paid the fee and b-lined it out the door. By the time Linda turned around to give the guy his change, he was already gone. As it turns out,

Detective Bob knew the guy. Apparently, he had 'sent him away' a few years earlier. Jeez, no wonder the guy freaked. I asked Bob what the guy had done, but he could not tell me. I would have asked him myself if he would have ever shown his face in the shop again - which he did not.

It's a Sham

Over my lifetime, I have really come to understand the importance of a good doctor. When you need a procedure done, have an illness, or have children, your level of comfort is dependent on the relationship and trust you have in your doctor.

When my brother Richie was diagnosed with cancer more than ten years ago, he became discouraged as he struggled to find a trustworthy, optimistic, and confident cancer specialist. The disease itself is obviously anxiety provoking, but not having confidence in the treatment you are receiving really can seem like the straw that will break the camel's back.

I'll never forget when Richie called me to tell me about this new doctor he had found who had given him a renewed sense of hope and determination to fight the disease. He told me the doctor's name was Sham. *Funny name*, I thought. I was, however, elated at the good news.

Not more than a week later, I was doing the hair of one of my long-time customers, Ron. We had been friends for some time and I always enjoyed our candid conversations. Not to toot my own horn, but he also loved the haircuts I gave him. On this particular day, we got to talking about my brother Richie and his whole situation. I was telling him about how discouraged my brother had been having had so much trouble finding a doctor that he liked. I told him about the new doctor that Richie absolutely adored. It was at this point when Ron looked at me in an inquisitive manner, and asked me what my brother's last name was. When I told him, he said that he knew Richie. He was Dr. Sham! I ask you what the odds are of this actually happening. Craziness. I did not even know Ron was a doctor, let alone my brother's cancer doctor. Sometimes fate is funny, no? Then again, I guess the *best* must have a natural ability to sniff each other out.

Seriously, though, Ron is the best. He is brilliant in the treatment he provides my brother. He is dedicated, optimistic, yet realistic. We are all grateful to have him as a friend and professional confidant.

This whole incident happened more than eleven years ago, now, and Richie is doing great, and Ron's hair still looks fabulous. I just hope that my brother's success is not dependent on the hair of the good doctor-because if something were to happen to me, Dr. Sham would have to go to Linda by default. Eeks!

To whom it may Concern

Last year I received a letter from a dissatisfied customer (it's rare, but it happens). It read as follows:

Dear Pat,

I was told yesterday that you are the owner of the Progressive Barber Shop. I came to the Progressive yesterday because I was looking for a barber shop that is interesting and where I could get a good haircut. Unfortunately, although the shop is interesting, I am very dissatisfied with my haircut. Before the haircut, the barber and I agreed that not too much would be taken off, because I didn't want my hair too short. Nonetheless, my hair is now much shorter than I want it to be. She offered not to charge me, but I paid her twenty dollars because I felt she had done the work, although not to my satisfaction. When I got home, I realized that she had significantly raised my hair line in the back, which I definitely do not like. Had I realized this when I was in the shop yesterday, I would not have paid her. Under the circumstances, I think it is appropriate to refund my $20.

Thank you for your review and consideration of this issue.

Bob Smith

After some deliberation with the girls and my husband, I responded as follows:

Dear Bob,

We are delighted that you found our shop interesting as so many of our customers do. As for your haircut, it would help me a great deal if you could tell me exactly how much of your hair was taken off. With that information, *I* could more easily tell *you* whether your hair is now shorter than you want it to be. We are also concerned about the $20 refund that you requested. We charge $16 for a haircut. Why did you leave a tip?

Thank You,

Patricia Parker

I never got to send the response to old Bob because the very next morning he called me at the shop. Bottom line: after a brief conversation, I offered him a haircut on the house if he were to come back in. I have not seen him yet, but the IOU is still in my barber's drawer.

Fortunately, for every unhappy customer there are fifty more that *are* happy. I received *this* letter from a very nice young man. It read:

Alan Wilder
567 Elm Street

Rochester, NY

Dear Owner,

Last June I went to your barbershop with my dad to get a haircut. When we left, your great service was the main thing on my mind. Your employees are very friendly and good hair cutters too! When we entered we were greeted warmly and ushered to seats right away. While our haircuts were being executed I talked with the friendly staff and listened to the radio. Then, after admiring our fresh haircuts, I got three free gum balls (the highlight of my day!). Visiting your barbershop was a great experience for me with the friendly atmosphere and a good haircut. I hope to go to the Progressive Barber shop again and I will beg my parents to take me there!

Sincerely,

Alan Wilder

    Alan made my day. I had to write him back and thank him for his kind words. I wrote:

Progressive Barber Shop

1122 Monroe Ave.

Rochester, New York 14624

Master Barber / Owner

Phone: 585.413.6290

September 1, 2008

Hi Alan!

I just received your nice letter and I have to tell you that I was very touched, not only by your kind words but by your taking the time to write me. I'm so happy that you enjoyed your visit to the barber shop. It means a lot to me and my employees. We really try to not only give good haircuts but also to make the clients feel welcomed. Letters like yours makes me feel a sense of accomplishment and makes me strive to continue to be the best. We all at the barber shop want to thank you for your thoughtfulness. The world needs more people like you. I look forward to seeing you for your next haircut. I'll have a whole new shipment of fresh gumballs! Alan, when you come in, please give me some kind of hint as to who you are. I have so many customers that I get sometimes confused as to who's who. I really want to give you a big hug!

Sincerely,

Patricia L. Parker

What a sweetheart. Pooh on you, Bob!

Old Man Dan and the Model Convict

Young actor revels in hair-raising act

Fifteen-year-old Dan Gilbert loves the theater so much that he'd do anything for a role.

This week "anything" meant shaving the top of his head for his role as the elderly Mr. Lundy in Brighton High School's musical production of *Brigadoon*, which opens today.

Gilbert

Dan willingly sacrificed for his craft to achieve that balding look for his 80-ish character. At first, show director Larry Dugan "emphatically said, 'No way,'" according to the freshman.

The baby-powder-in-the-hair look, however, just made Dan's dirty blond hair look pink under the lights.

So Dugan and Julene Gilbert, Dan's mother and *Brigadoon* costume coordinator, agreed to the shave-off.

Dan and his father, Barry Gilbert, went to the Progressive Barber Shop in Rochester to do the deed. "You never notice how cold Rochester is until you have nothing on top of your head," joked Dan, whose older sister Cara is also in the production.

Dan feared that the balding would prompt others to tease him.

"Everyone thinks it's cool, everyone thinks it's phat," he said. "They want to rub my head for luck."

The musical will begin at 7:30 p.m. today and tomorrow and 3 p.m. Sunday. Tickets are $8 for seniors and students and $10 for adults for the night performances. Matinee tickets are $6 for students and seniors and $8 for adults. For details, call 242-5047.

As I stated before, I have been asked to do all sorts of haircuts over the years. One stands out in my mind, in particular. It was the only time in all my years when a kid with a full head of beautiful hair asked me to make him look like a balding older man. I have had balding older men come in and ask me to make them look young again, but never the other way around! It's ludicrous! The kid's name was Dan. I had been his barber since he was a little child. He was going to take part in a play, and was playing the role of an older man. I guess nobody could accuse him of not committing to the part.

Luckily for Dan, there happened to be a man in the next chair whose hairline had naturally taken the shape that he wanted to adopt. I asked the man if I could use his head as a guideline and he agreed. So I did. When I was through, Dan's hair was identical to the balding man. It was fantastic. Dan was happy, I was relieved that I didn't massacre his scalp, and the man got a kick out of it, too.

It was kind of ironic that a short time later, the man who had lent us his hairline as a blueprint went to jail for tax evasion. He may have been a good head model, but he was no sort of role model for young Dan.

In One Ear...

One Saturday morning a few years ago, Ro came into work complaining about an earache that had kept her up all night. She said she had already gone to the doctor about it, and had been on antibiotics for days; but, she had experienced no relief from her pain. You didn't know this, but when it comes to treating random illnesses, Linda and I are like Witch Doctors. We put our heads together and came up with a whole assortment of unconventional, impractical…and perhaps *unwise* remedies.

One of us suggested first that we try blowing cigarette smoke gently into Ro's ear. I forget who suggested this one, but I am sure the other one of us thought it was a grand idea! It was not. By the time we realized that our idea wasn't working, we were half a pack closer to emphysema. And boy, how bad Ro smelled having had a half pack of cigarette smoke blown directly into her hair.

Another idea we had was to heat up a sack of beans and put the warmness of the bag on the side of Ro's head. Another bad idea. We put the beans in the microwave for a bit too long and ended up giving Ro second degree burns on her earlobe. This idea was a bit more successful when you consider how pain displacement works. Ro would probably disagree with me, though.

It was about then that Linda started referring back to her extensive knowledge of Chinese folk medicine. There was a device that she had heard of that could apparently suck the sickness out of the body if placed in the ear canal. We called around some of the local Chinese shops, and lo and behold, we found what we were looking for. How funny I must have looked buying what looked like a gigantic Chinese finger trap intended for curing matters of the ear in the same store here Grandpa bought Gizmo in *Gremlins*. Remember? It was unnecessarily dark and spooky.

Anyway, I get back to the shop and proceeded to read directions written in Chinglish. The way I interpreted it, we had to light one end of the tube on fire, and when it began to smoke, we should stick the unlit end into the distressed ear. One thing I understood perfectly clearly in the directions was that when the tube burned down about halfway, we were supposed to hear a crackling sound coming from the ear itself. The smoke was supposed to suck the infection out. Oh, God, how Linda and I were intrigued.

It is still unbelievable to me that Ro started feeling relief instantaneously. Our kooky idea actually worked. Linda and I felt like the ladies from Grey's Anatomy (but older, and less attractive). It was appropriate though. Did you know that in the days of old, barbers commonly doubled as surgeons and dentists? I already have a couple ideas up my sleeve if ever Ro comes down with a toothache.

What grosses you out?

The amount of bodily fluids a barber comes into contact with on a regular basis is staggering. One day a kid passes by on the sidewalk and hocks a loogie on the window resembling the inside of an apple fritter in both color and consistency; the next day I arrive at the shop to find a puddle of chicken wing barf on the stoop in front of the barbershop door. I try to pour water on it to dilute the grossness, but I have to stop as I, myself, am unable to avoid vomiting. I didn't even put a dent in the mess. This was a case where I had to call the landlords. They did, after all, also own the bar that the puking man must have crawled out from early that same morning.

Both these stories, as gross as they were, pale in comparison to the King of All putridity. An old man named Andy comes into the shop as a first time customer and tells me he has to use the bathroom before he sits down to have his haircut. Twenty minutes later, I am beginning to get a little concerned, but Andy does eventually come out. I do notice a little pee stain on the crotch of his plaid slacks, but it's no big deal; I let it slide to spare the old man any embarrassment. After he left I decided to check the bathroom. I figured if he couldn't drain his hose before he pulled up his pants, what other sacrifices was he making as far as his sanitation was concerned? Sadly, I was right.

It looked like a machine exploded in a peanut butter melting factory (if there is such a thing)! Shit was everywhere *except* the toilet. The old man must have spent 5 minutes spraying the room with shit, and another twenty trying to hide his catastrophe. Maybe he had not noticed that his feces had splashed waist-high on the bathroom wall. Oh God, what a foul stench there was.

I felt bad for the old guy for about 8 seconds, which is when I began the cleanup process. I Lysoled everything from the walls, to the mirror, to the seat, to the trashcan. The only thing I did not soak in chemicals was the throw rug beneath the john. Some things are better off replaced.

Not that I would have ever brought it up to the old man, but I never did see him again. I can only surmise that the first and only visit he ever had at the Progressive Barbershop *pooped* him out so much, he could not bear to return. Pun definitely intended.

Patties Little Helpers

Having loyal customers is second fiddle to having great friends; and more often than not, my most loyal customers *are* my greatest friends. Success as a business owner is obviously dependent on your customer base, but friends are of utmost importance in that they can help you out of what may seem like impossible situations.

I recall one of those record-breaking days when I was pumping out haircuts like gasoline, finishing two or three cuts every hour from open to closing time. On this particularly busy day at the shop, one of the cacti that adorn the front window finally outsized the pot it had sat in for several years, tipping over the sitting chairs, not only making a god awful mess, but eliminating any semblance of a waiting area. Not good on one of the busiest days of my life. The kicker was that I was so busy, I could not even take the time to rebalance the plant; and, even if I did find the time, it was too heavy for me to move on my own. Lo and behold, in walks my friend Dom. Without so much as a 'Hello,' he walks over to the cactus and sets it back upright for me. But that's not all! He cleans up the mess that was made, and even goes as far as to replant the prickerbush in a bigger pot. I have not mentioned that the needles on this particular cactus are about two inches long and as sharp as tacks. Dom did not even hesitate, however; basically risking his life to help me out. Needless to say, I did not charge him for his appointment despite his objections.

In Rochester, winter is the best time of the year to have your friends around. Because I am usually at the shop for many hours every day, there have been times where the plows have visited and revisited the Avenue, and at the end of the day I have discovered my car buried under three feet of snow or more. It is at times like this, when I love my little friend, Givonne. Givonne is the boy who lives on the second floor behind the shop. He is now in High School, but as a child Givonne used to come down to help me out at the end of the day, whether to help me dig my car out of the snow, or to help me sweep and vacuum the shop at the end of the day. Even now, whenever Givonne comes in for a visit, he asks me if there is anything he can do to lend me a hand. I wish there were more young men like him in the world; it really would be a better place.

I could go on and on about how grateful I am for the help that all my friends have lent me over the years. Whether it be that they went the store to get me a pop, or went into the basement to fix a blown fuse, or changed a light bulb that I could not reach, or drove me to the mechanic's shop to pick up my car, my friends are, and continue to be, extraordinarily wonderful and selfless. Thank you friends. I only hope that you feel as if I have earned your generosity.

Isn't that sign missing an I?

I have repeatedly referred to Linda, my friend and colleague, and her wacky shenanigans. There is one story that sticks with me that personifies Linda's whole personality.

Linda and her husband Mike live in a town in Southern Ney York called Prattsburg, where life is lived at a snail's pace. Prattsburgians think nothing of taking a day off from work to do things like baling hay, hunting, and tending to livestock.

Linda comes into the shop one day, laughing her head off as she walked through the door. When I asked her what was so funny, she explained that she and Mike had been driving down the road the previous night, and passed by the Prattsburg High School. There was a sign in front of the building that read:

School will be closed for **MLKing Day**

Her and her husband found this to be not only amusing, but *udderly* ridiculous. She went on and on about how funny she thought it was that school would be cancelled for something as nineteenth century as 'milking day.' Do you see where I might be going, yet?

As her discussion continued, the guy in my chair has an epiphany. He says to me softly, so as not to embarrass my ignorant friend, "Martin Luther King Day." You see, school was cancelled for *MLKing* Day, but it had nothing to do with cows. It was Martin Luther King Day! Linda and Mike had thought the sign was missing the letter *I*. I could not contain myself. I laughed so hard, I peed. The whole shop was rolling as Linda turned beet red.

Anyway, the next day I receive an envelope from Jim, who had been in the chair during the whole unbelievable story that Linda had told the day before. I open the envelope and inside there is a picture of Dr. King holding up four of his fingers in the air. The caption below the picture read:

"This is how one grabs an utter when milking a cow."

Just for a second, I'd like to have the opportunity to see the world through Linny's eyes. I imagine it looks eerily similar to Dorothy's Wonderland.

Step 2: Insert Foot in Mouth

I take pride in saying that most of my customers would come to my defense if ever it were necessary. I never thought that I would have to return the favor someday. Well that is exactly what happened when this strange, nervous, confused-looking woman came into the shop one afternoon. All of these adjectives led me to one though – get her out of here ASAP!

Apparently, she had been on her way to the eyeglasses store, but had gotten off the bus at the wrong stop, and she was now completely lost on the wrong end of the avenue. My friend Tim was in the chair at the time.

Being the motherly type that I am, I began going through the yellow pages, trying to find an eyeglasses place on Monroe Avenue, but to no avail. The next best solution?

Without thinking, I blurted, "Hey, I bet Tim would drive you down the street to look for the place!" As soon as the suggestion came out of my mind, I didn't like it. Oops. Sometimes my mouth overrides my brain; this was one of those times.

But, the cat was already out of the bag. And, after that moment, the woman would not let Tim off the hook I had so generously hung him on. He tried politely to decline my invitation, but it was hopeless, he was stuck.

When Tim's haircut was finished, the parasitic woman basically forced herself on him, pushing him to his car so she could get a ride. I felt so guilty about putting my friend in this position, that I felt I had to see it out with him.

I closed the shop and jumped into the backseat of his car, telling him that I wanted to come to because there was someplace I needed to go, as well. There was no place I needed to go. I was afraid this woman would pull a gun on my friend, or cry out rape as he drove her to her destination, so I felt I had to be there with him. Just in case.

We did get her there without incident – Thank God. As soon as she was out of the car, we high-tailed it out of there without so much as a 'See Ya.' I apologized up and down to Tim, realizing that I was to blame for the entire situation.

A good lesson did come out of the ordeal, though. Bottom line: Leave the fruits and nuts for the baker; they make better cakes than passengers.

Six Degrees of Separation

At a glance, Rochester might not appear to be a city whose population schmoozes with celebrity-type people. Living here almost my whole life, I have come to understand that this is not the case at all. Over the years, I have come to collect a generous amount of celebrity photographs that have been brought to me by my customers. I put many of these photographs on the shop walls, and they have proven to be great conversation starters with newly acquired clients.

I have one photograph of Katie Couric posing with two of my favorite regulars, Dale and his wife Louise. I also love the picture of another one of my customers posing with Courtney Cox and Jennifer Anniston at a *Friends* Christmas party. All three of them have beers in their hands. It's great!

A girl who used to work at the shop is sister-in-law to Brian Gionta, of the New Jersey Devils. We have a great autographed photograph of him holding the much desired Stanley Cup.

My friend Sheldon brought me my all-time favorite picture, though. I like this one picture in particular because the celebrity in it apparently is not keen on having his picture taken in public. Lucky for me, Sheldon had a way in. Sheldon's grandfather was one of the founders of the renowned Hickey Freedman Clothing Company, which provides some of the best threads in the world. Shel always looks like he just stepped out of *Vogue* Magazine. I might not ever be able to afford their clothes, but this is not to say that I have not capitalized on their success.

Shel told me one day that he was going to Texas to take measurements on one of the most popular athletes in the world. I told him that he absolutely had to get a picture to bring back to me. He assured me that he would find a way. And he did.

Shel told the popular golfer that he needed to get a picture of him wearing the suit so that the tailors back home could see what the final product should look like. So hanging on my wall is a picture of Shel, alongside **Tiger Woods**, measuring the inseam of his thousand dollar slacks. The picture is even signed on the back. It reads:

***"To Pattie, the best barber in the world.
Sincerely, Tiger."***

I have been told that the signature looks an awful lot like my handwriting, but I'll never come clean about it. It can only surmise that Tiger and I must have similar penmanship.

Administrative Cuts

Aside from accumulating pictures of celebrities through relationships with my customers, I have also befriended real-life local celebrities through the barbershop. One of my oldest customers and good friends is Rochester city Mayor Bob Duffy. Every Saturday, Bob would come into the shop to have Linda trim him up for upcoming city council meetings and local television interviews.

Over the years, I have grown to really admire Mayor Duffy both for his character, and for his determination to better the city he shares with so many. I do not admire his position, I have to say. The stress must be unbearable at times. Between the crime, the city budget, and the general politics of it all, I just can't imagine all the work that goes into being city Mayor.

That being said, I have to admit that *I* have not made his job any easier over the years. You might recall the whole NET situation that I talked about earlier. Well, Bob was a very involved 'mediator' to that whole situation. I'm not sure if it was appropriate of me to lobby for the small business coalition as Bob sat in the chair beside me with sharp instruments buzzing and snipping around his eyes and ears, but then again, little of what I do is appropriate.

As is so often the case in politics, after his election Bob slightly modified his position concerning the NET and the Certificate of Use; he also changed barbershops. I understand, though. If I were him, I wouldn't want to face my big mouth either.

I was not devastated by any of these things. What I was upset about was the heat I was getting concerning the mayors hair! Whoever he switched to apparently gave a 'different' kind of haircut. Customers would come in left and right, asking me which one of my girls had been doing Duffy's hair. I explained that Bob no longer came to Progressive, so none of my girls were to blame. *Jeez,* I though, *how bad could it look?*

Let me tell you. Bob Lonsberry, a local radio personality actually talked about it on his talk-radio morning show. From what I heard, Lonsberry even got to digging on the barber, never mentioning me, specifically. I decided that I was taking too much flack for someone else's bad, so I decided to take matters into my own hands.

I emailed Lonsberry, filling him in the situation leading up to Duffy's leaving the Progressive Barbershop. I had to defend myself, after all. I was not going to continue taking bashes for work I had not done. I closed my email with a post script, suggesting that maybe the mayor should suck it up and return to Progressive.

Within a few weeks, lo and behold, guess who Lonsberry has on his morning show. That's right! And again, the discussion about the hair came up. Apparently, Mr. Lonsberry had shared the email I sent him with the Mayor, because the shop was mentioned by name in the conversation. Hey, you can't blame me for trying to protect the integrity of my business, can you?

Bob never has come back, but I don't harness any ill will toward him. Fess up though, Mr. Mayor, are you cutting your *own* hair?

Professor, what's another word for Pirate's Treasure? I think it's Booty-that's what it is.

In a business as small as mine, everybody has different responsibilities around the shop in order to keep things tidy. Linda has the wonderful task of cleaning the bathroom; Ro sweeps the floors, vacuums the carpets and empties the garbage. I maintain the plants. It's a simple system that works.

A few months ago, I arrived at the shop feeling especially devious. I thought it would be funny to mess with Linda this particular day - again. Before anyone else arrived at the shop, I couldn't help but notice that Linda's favorite leather boots were sitting lonely beneath the customer coat rack. Linda was going to have to pay for being late on this day, for sure. I thought, wouldn't it be a riot if her boots were in the garbage when Linda came in to work? I thought so, so that is where I put them.

Unfortunately for all of us, by the time the girls arrived to work that day, the shop had already begun to fill up, and business was bumping. I didn't notice that Ro had begun cleaning as soon as she walked in the door. I was busy, after all. It is also important to note how much of a cleaning machine Ro is. We call her a cleaning *Ro*bot. She will throw out anything in her path once she gets going. And that's just what she did.

A few hours into the day, we finally began to slow down, and had a chance to shoot the breeze. Ro asked Linda why on earth she threw out her favorite boots; she wore them almost every day, after all. Of course, Linda had no idea what

Ro was talking about. Two minutes later, Lin went into a state of panic. I'm rolling at this point. I'm laughing so hard, I did not even feel guilty about what I had done.

Picture Ro crawling halfway into the dumpster behind the shop, fishing through a week's worth of rancid garbage, trying to find the bag with the boots, and excavate them using an aluminum broomstick. By the way, a dumpster is not a good place to find relief from the heat of a ninety degree day. Just ask Ro. A true Kodak moment.

It took a week to air out those boots; and they never were the same after that. They had turned an earthy green color, and always had a bit of foulness about them. I'm just glad Linda had the heart not to but the boots on when she put her foot up my ass.

A Fine Mess I'm In

I thought that I would close my story with a good anecdote about how it is owning a business in Rochester. This happened just a few weeks ago, as 2007 was coming to a close.

In walks a state business inspector on the prowl, looking for any number of reasons to cite me for infractions. This guy really must have been having a bad day, because he got me good.

Now, usually when these inspectors come around, they cite you and you (the business owner) are allotted a certain amount of time to remedy the infraction. All you have to do is send in the appropriate documentation that the problem has been fixed. This situation was unique, however. As is the case in a bar, where you are required to display your liquor license, a barber is required to display her licenses. I have three of them. I have a barbering license in the same frame as my New York State License, and I have my cosmetology license, which is in a separate frame.

The citation I received was for not having a picture to go with each of my three licenses. Talk about nit-picky. But, whatever; the guy was there to do a job, and he did it. Good for him.

Anyway, two days later, I had fixed the problem and was getting ready to send in the evidence that I had taken care of it, when I received a letter telling me that I was already being charged a one hundred dollar fine. Huh? Of course they gave me option as to how I could deal with the situation.

I could either pay the fine, and that would be that; or, I could contest it in court in Buffalo in front of a judge, losing a full day's work and having to pay for the gas to get there. And, there was no guarantee that I would win in court, anyway. Great options, I know. I decided that none of these options were for me, so I made my own option.

I wrote a letter of complaint to the city newspaper, to the attorney general, and to the governor of New York. Yes, I did all of this because of a measly hundred dollar fine. The truth is I am sick of working long, hard hours just to have my money extorted by a state that cannot manage a budget. Damn the man, I say! It seems that this situation might make a good opening chapter in the sequel.

T.G.I.F.

At the end of a long, tiring week, Friday's become "let your hair down day". The client's are often offered something to drink or even a shot of Bailey's Irish Cream with their coffee. It more often turns into a ten hour day, telling jokes, chillin' and discussing different topics. One time, a very good client and friend of mine decided to whip his jeans down and show us his Buffalo Bills logo he had tattooed on his thigh, next to his Simpson's boxer shorts. That was one hairy Buffalo. Of course, that was like opening Pandora's Box. Everyone had to show off their tattoos. I showed off my little ladybug on my ankle (what a wild lady) only to have everyone ask how I got "that cigarette burn". I was so blown away that soon after, I went back to the tattoo joint and had a leaf drawn around my bug. I have to agree it did look a lot better. My husband suggested that I have it drawn on my boob, but figured it would eventually end up around my ankle anyway. Growing old sucks!

The Move

It's March, 2008. I've decided to move my insane asylum into a new and bigger facility. The influx of new nuts has flourished and I have realized the need for more space. With the move came new custom made solid oak cabinets, a beautiful counter top and a unique solid oak containment that was specially made for all my array of cacti. My son Gabriel contributed many hours of hard work and his talents to make this happen for his mama, as did my son Nathaniel who edited my book. Let's not forget all that my hubby contributed to the cause also. He made from scratch a super roomy storage room and a retainment wall so that women might be able to have a little privacy from the men when having their hair done. I really felt that this might be a good idea considering the sometimes crude behavior that I seem to stir up. He also transformed an inside outhouse into a very respectable place where the customers could do their business without the fear of cooties attacking them. Believe me that was a real possibility had you seen the condition of the bathroom. The whole place needed a face lift. The first week that I opened for business the front door fell off, on Regina! Ro, quick thinking as she is, managed to pull it off poor little Gina before she got squished to death. That was a month or so after she had knee replacement on her broken old body. Ro, you're our hero! My landlord still is deciding who broke the 200 pound door, me or God. Chalk that five hundred and forty dollar bill to fate. KARMA Kenny. You might want to look it up in the dictionary. Linda and Sue have since retired after years of abusing their feet and backs (and minds).

With them, go many wonderful memories and friendships that were built among the many loyal clients. I will very much miss them both as co-workers but we will always remain close friends in our personal lives. I have since hired a new staff along with Ro and myself. I'd like to introduce to you Regina and Lori. Regina used to work at the barber shop four years ago and apparently couldn't get enough of the craziness that she left behind so she's baaack! Lori I stole from a shop down the street. It took me awhile to break her in to the insanity that goes with the job but I triumphed. They both enjoy working with both men and women's hair. Does this mean that I will perhaps change my evil, nasty ways or possibly clean up my potty mouth? NOT!!! As the back cover says…it's a barber shop, NOT a salon! Welcome to the Progressive girls. The best is yet to come.

Man or Beast

Last month a rather bazaar thing happened. (Are you surprised?) A big 6 foot, 5 inch client came in for a haircut with a tale of shear horror. He was visiting his cabin in the southern tier a week earlier when what he thought was a nightmare, turned out to be real. He discovered a 250 pound bear trying to get into his cabin through the front door. When the bear spotted John standing there, axe in one hand and poop in his trousers, the big black intruder decided he would like him for dinner, and not as a guest. As John made a dash for his truck, the bear followed, grunting and making frightening sounds. John was forced to defend himself or become bear poop the next day. Can you figure out who won that battle?

Throughout the telling of his account with the bear, which held us in total amazement, I couldn't help noticing the Wegman's bag on his lap. I casually asked what was in it. Out comes the bear claw still attached to the leg – frozen solid. The three of us flew in different directions screaming like my husband does in the morning when he first looks into the mirror after fighting with his three pillows all night long. The girls were pale white and visibly freaked out. I snapped a picture of John and his trophy, fully aware that it could be the mother of all my conversational pieces.

For the rest of the day my nerves were a bit frayed and it took awhile to compose myself. I had visions through the rest of the day of a big,

Think these stories aren't true? Here's John and his bear.

black hairy paw on my shoulder, in my drawer, even following me to the bathroom. There were paws all over the place. I found myself at a loss of confidence with my scissors, especially around meaty parts like ears, noses and lips. Remember when I said that it's not a good thing to nip a nose? I meant it!

Just Recently…

I 'm just about ready to end my tales here, but I feel that it would be a sin to deprive all you beautiful people of my last unexpected story that happened just the other day. It's Halloween, 2008 and as usual all the girls wore costumes to work. Regina was dressed as a seventy's hippie with an afro to kill for. Lori was a Rastafarian and yours truly, was the wicked witch of the west, mole and all.

Jan the mail lady delivered our mail, screeching and making ghoulish sounds such as those made by one who's about to go postal.

Clay is filling his mouth with candy in between naps while others were indulging in cider, doughnut holes and Halloween fun.

Meanwhile, I was having a hell of a time cutting hair because my fake witch's nose was making me breathe differently. This odd breathing was fogging up my glasses. In came my client Ed with a six pack in his hand. I put a drape on him and began to cut his hair. It was like a bad dream. There I stood with Ed's 6 inch tail in my hand that took him 5 years to grow! How did that happen? I found myself asking that very question – *very* carefully. All he kept saying was, "you're kidding, right?" Thank goodness he had consumed enough beer to mellow a herd of raging bulls. I now have a new tail on my wall… he has a new hairdo. Happy Halloween Ed, better luck next year.

In Closing

I'm now entering my 34th year of business at the Progressive Barbershop. I have three wonderful girls working for me, a quaint home-style barber shop and very successful business with a clientele that most people would kill for. Aside from the street urchin exposing himself, Karen getting punched out by a whacko when she tried to help him up after he fell, me almost getting arrested for throwing a NET (neighborhood empowerment team) inspector out of my shop because he was an ass, I wouldn't trade one day of my barbering years for all the tea in China. The rewards have been plentiful. Friends are customers, customers are friends, and for every story of sadness and frustration, there are ten of hope and joy. How much better does it get!

■■■■■■■■■■■■■■■■■■■■■■■■■■■■■■■■■■■■■

Afterword

In today's hectic world, people need a place to escape to where they can *do* whatever, *act* however, and *be* whatever they want. That place is the Progressive Barbershop. The preceding anecdotes are all true stories (with names adjusted so as not to offend anyone) about only a few of the people who have come to adopt the shop as a neighborhood hangout.

To me, the shop is a home away from home; to others, it is a place to hang their hat, have a hot cup of coffee, and it is a place where they can check their stressors, whatever they might be, at the door. And all this for the price of a haircut. I hope that having read about some of my experiences over the past 30+ years, you entertain the idea of stopping in for an experience of your own. I promise we'll leave the door open for you. Come on in and join us; there is no need to call ahead. We'll be expecting you.